PURE CORK

MICHAEL LENIHAN

To

Pat

Best wishes

Michael Lenihan

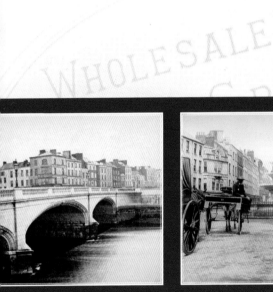

MERCIER PRESS

IRISH PUBLISHER – IRISH STORY

Contents

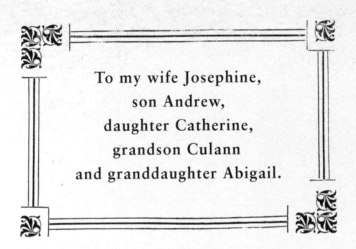

To my wife Josephine,
son Andrew,
daughter Catherine,
grandson Culann
and granddaughter Abigail.

Acknowledgements

This book would not have materialised without the assistance and kindness of the following people: Denis Lenihan for his wonderful insight into the geographical locations of Cork city; Anita Lenihan and Tony Lenihan for their interest and helpful suggestions; Harry Ormond for skilfully photographing the Cork tokens within the book; Terry Atridge for her professional scanning of the old stereo views and glass lantern slides; Niamh Twomey, Heritage Officer for Cork City Council and Ciara Brett, city archaeologist, whose assistance proved invaluable; Cork City Council, who provided a grant that aided in the digitising and archiving of some of the early images; Lesley Roberts for donating duplicate invoices from his personal collection; Dr Richard T. Cooke, Dr Donal Ó Drisceoil of UCC, Antoin O'Callaghan, Ronnie Herlihy, Pat Poland and the South Parish Historical Society, whose interest and encouragement is greatly appreciated.

A special word of thanks to the staff of Mercier Press whose unwavering support produced this magnificent book: Catherine Twibill for her expertise in designing and formatting every image; Wendy Logue, who typed and made sense of the captions; Patrick Crowley, whose marketing skills are invaluable; Sharon O'Donovan, who was always helpful at the other end of the telephone; Mary Feehan and Clodagh Feehan for their support publishing this tome.

Last but not least my wife Josephine, without whose help and tolerance this project would ever have seen the light of day.

Introduction

How did this book come about? Well it did not happen overnight. It was many years ago that I first became interested in Cork history. As a small boy my inquisitive mind was fascinated by my father Denis Lenihan's stories of old Cork. My eyes used to light up listening to his tales of Cork people and places, which all came to life when he recounted these stories of a different time. As I grew up I became more and more interested in collecting memorabilia of those times. I started with stamps, but I quickly became addicted to collecting Cork postcards and I was soon well and truly hooked.

I first started collecting postcards at the age of thirteen when I discovered a stamp and coin dealer, Malcolm Moss, located on French's Quay. I can remember he paid two shillings and sixpence for soaking 1,000 stamps from pieces of envelopes and drying them on newspapers. Well I handed him 2,000 stamps and was paid the princely sum of five shillings for my efforts. But I could not leave the shop without spending my loot on twelve black and white Cork postcards, complete with their very own advertising envelope. I continued collecting until I became interested in the fairer sex, and when I married my collecting passion was put on hold.

Years ago my good wife Josephine suggested in passing that I start collecting again. Well, being an obedient husband, I did as I was told. Every Saturday morning was spent going to collector fairs and antique auctions. I would arrive home with a customary box of cakes and a new clutch of Cork postcards. Tea, cakes and postcards were quaffed, eaten and

perused, in that order, by Josephine and myself. The collection grew and grew until I discovered that there were other forms of images out there – rare stereo views, glass lantern slides and original photographs. Stereo views consist of twin images mounted on a card and viewed through a special viewer called a stereoscope. These images predate the postcard and the earliest stereo view reproduced in this book is dated to the 1850s. Glass lantern slides consist of a large negative (often hand coloured) sandwiched between two pieces of glass. These slides, sometimes called magic lantern slides, certainly live up to their name – they are just magic.

Unfortunately, in the early 1960s and 1970s many old things were thrown out to make way for the new. Old postcards, glass lantern slides and stereo views had no place in the new fashion-conscious world. Old established firms such as Guy & Co., one of the greatest exponents of photography and publisher of local views, inadvertently disposed of all of their archival material. Examples of their local views are now quite rare. I had to smile some years ago when I saw a sign outside a local antique shop: 'Buy what your grandmother threw away'.

My collection represents only a minute part of what existed. These are moments frozen in time, which need to be preserved and promoted. Most of the images in this book have not been reproduced before. I hope that my love and passion for Cork history can be seen in this publication, which represents only a fraction of my collection of original pictures, postcards and literature relating to Cork city's rich history.

Michael Lenihan

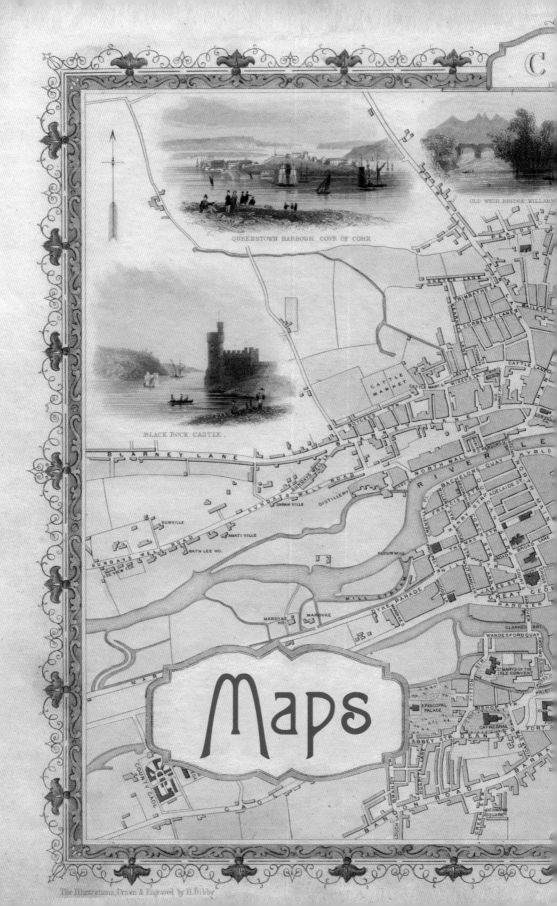

QUEENSTOWN HARBOUR, COVE OF CORK.

OLD WEIR BRIDGE, KILLARNEY

BLACK ROCK CASTLE.

Maps

The Illustrations Drawn & Engraved by H.Bibby

K.

MILITARY GRAVE YARD

MILITARY PRISON.

BLACK MILLER LANE

ST ANNS MARKET

POPES HILL

DISTILLERY

BARRACKS

BARRACKTON

YOUGHAL ROAD

MILITARY ROAD

COTTAGE ROAD

FEVER HOSPL

CAMP FIELD

ROPE WALK

AUDLEY PLACE

WELLINGTON ROAD

SUMMER

LOWER CLANMIRE ROAD

HARDWICK ST

PATRICKS P

SYDNEY PLA

ST PATRICKS R.C. CH

ALFRED STR.

COBURG ST

KING STREET

ST PATRICKS QUAY

PENROSES QUAY

STEAM PACKET OFFICE

CAMDEN QUAY

CH CHANNEL

COAL QUAY

LAVITTS QUAY

MERCHANTS QUAY

ANDERSONS QUAY

CUSTOM HOUSE

NAVIGATION WALK

FISH STR

LOWER GEORGES STR.

CORK BLACKROCK & PASSAGE RAILWAY TERMINUS

ST PATRICKS STREET

MAYLOR STR

VICTORIA PARK

GRAND PARADE

SOUTH MALL

LAPPS QUAY

ALBERT QUAY

VICTORIA ROAD

SOUTH CHANNEL

UNION QUAY

CORK & BANDON

RAILWAY STATION

NATIONAL EXHIBITION

GAS WORKS

HOLY TRINITY CHU.

RIVER LEE

SULLIVANS QUAY

CHARLOTTE QUAY

COPLEY STR.

GEORGES QUAY

STABLE

MARY STR

SOUTH TERRACE

WARRICK STR

DOUGLAS STR.

ABBEY

LANGFORD ROW

BLACKROCK ROAD

QUAKER RD

HIGH STR

BLARNEY CASTLE

The Plan Drawn & Engraved by J.Rapkin.

The earliest map of Cork reproduced here is the Tower Map and is taken from the *Irish Miscellany* (Cork 1796) printed by James Haly. Other maps include the extremely rare Stag Map from *c*. 1630, a 1714 plan of the city, a Cork International Exhibition map of 1903 and a map of the old Cork racecourse prior to the building of Henry Ford's factory. They show the development of the city over the centuries.

Previous Page: A fine hand-coloured plan of Cork from the 1850s by the great decorative mapmaker John Tallis. The map features four beautiful vignette illustrations of various landmarks: Blackrock Castle, Blarney Castle, Queenstown Harbour and the old Weir Bridge, Killarney.

The Tower Map was a sketch kept in the Tower of London and was dated to 1545. The original map could not be located in the 1940s and from that point the only widely known reproduction was printed in Tuckey's *Cork Remembrancer* of 1837. However, an earlier copy of this map, shown here, was in the possession of the printer James Haly, who reproduced it in the *Irish Miscellany* in 1796.

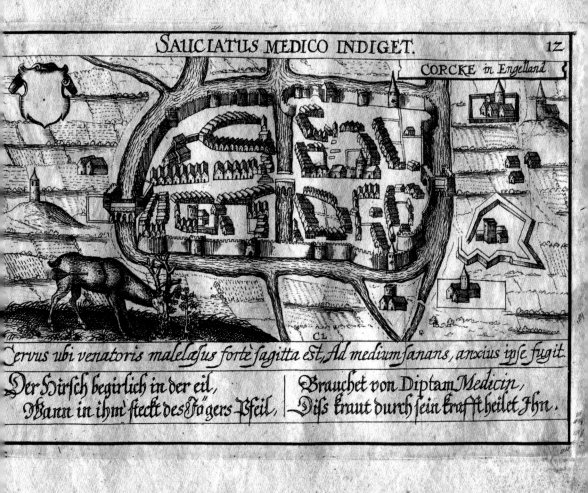

CORCKE *in Engelland*

CL

Cervus ubi venatoris malelaſus fortè ſagitta eſt, Ad medium ſanans, anxius ipſe fugit.

Der Hirsch begirlich in der eil, Brauchet von Diptam Medicin,
Wann in ihm' steckt des Jägers Pfeil. Diſs kraut durch sein krafft heilet Ihn.

This is a very rare map and it is known as the Stag Map because of the stag in the foreground. It is also entitled *Corcke in Engelland* and it was published by Denis Morden in his *Politici Thesauri Philo-Politici*, Nürnberg, *c*. 1630. It appears to be a variation of the Speed map of 1610. The Latin is translated as 'where by chance the stag has been badly injured by the hunters' arrow, half recovering he flees distressed'.

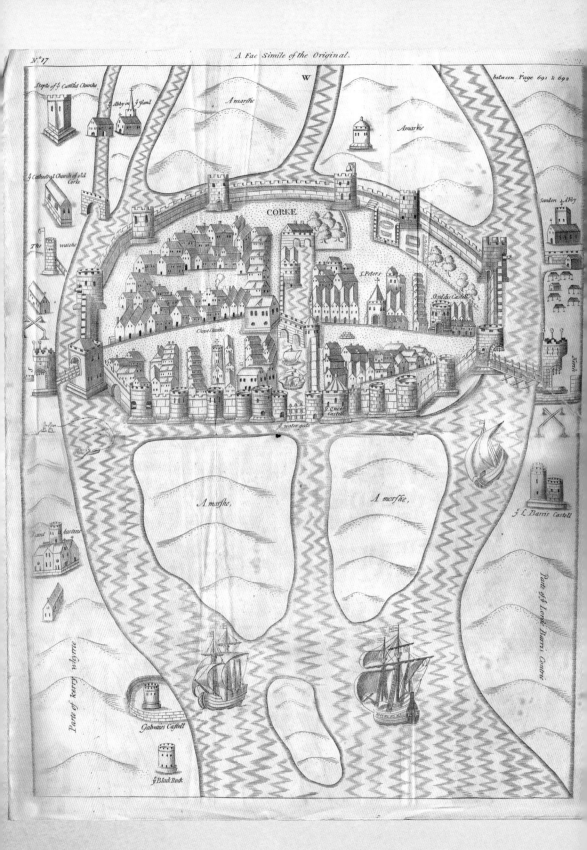

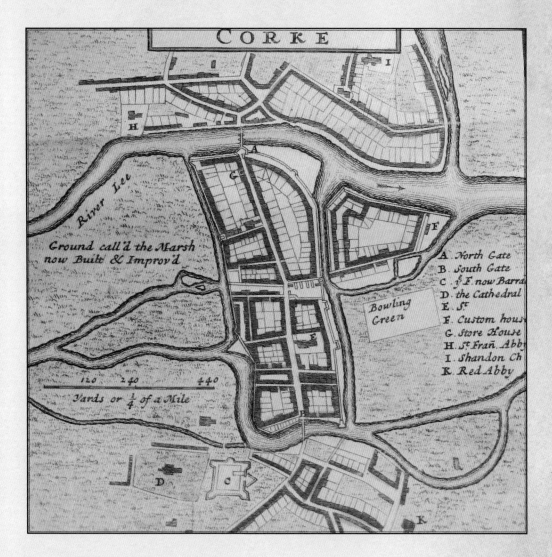

An inset plan of the city of Cork from a 1714 map of Ireland by Herman Moll. Herman Moll was a German-born London-based geographer, publisher, bookseller and globe maker. It is very similar to, and appears to be a variation of, Pratt's map of the city of Cork from *c.* 1708.

Opposite: This map is known as the *Pacata Hibernia* map, after the book of the same name which was printed in 1633. It predates this publication and dates to *c.* 1585–1600. Like many of its contemporaries it is mainly a sketch of the city, and it depicts the old walled city and its defences.

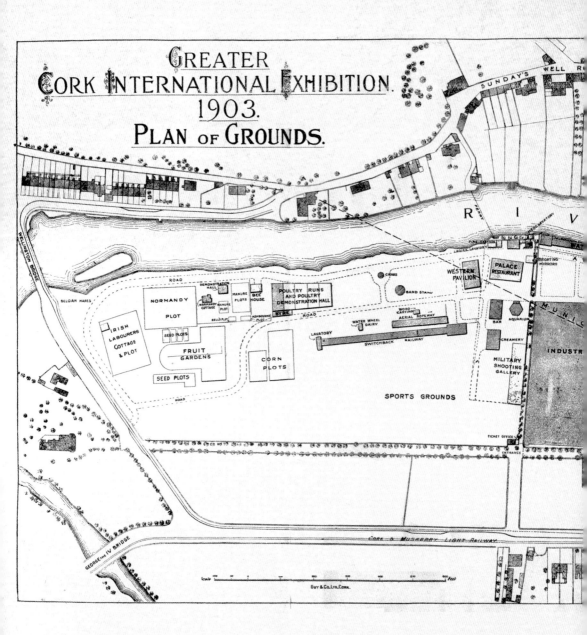

**GREATER CORK INTERNATIONAL EXHIBITION.
1903.
PLAN OF GROUNDS.**

This map shows the magnitude of the grounds of the Greater Cork Exhibition of 1903. The Industrial Hall, the largest building shown on the map, covered an area of 170,000 feet. Adjoining it was the Machinery Hall measuring 200 feet by 100 feet.

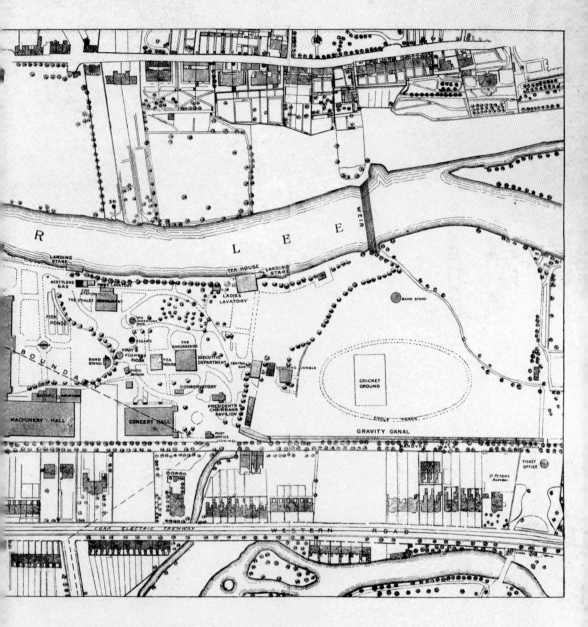

Overleaf: This street map of Cork in the form of a postcard dates to *c.* 1905 and was engraved by the firm of Bartholomew & Co. It shows the tram and railway lines which traversed the city, and the inset has a nice vignette of Patrick Street.

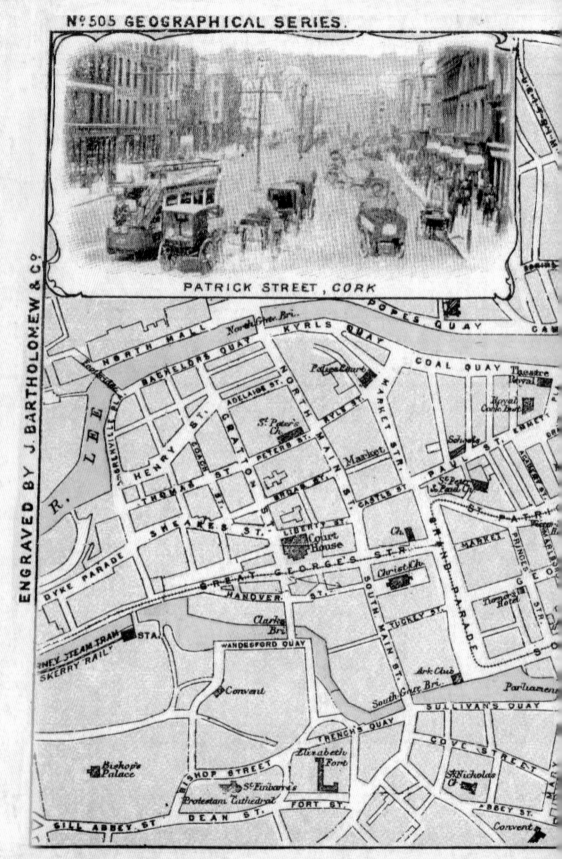

PATRICK STREET, CORK

ENGRAVED BY J. BARTHOLOMEW & Cº.

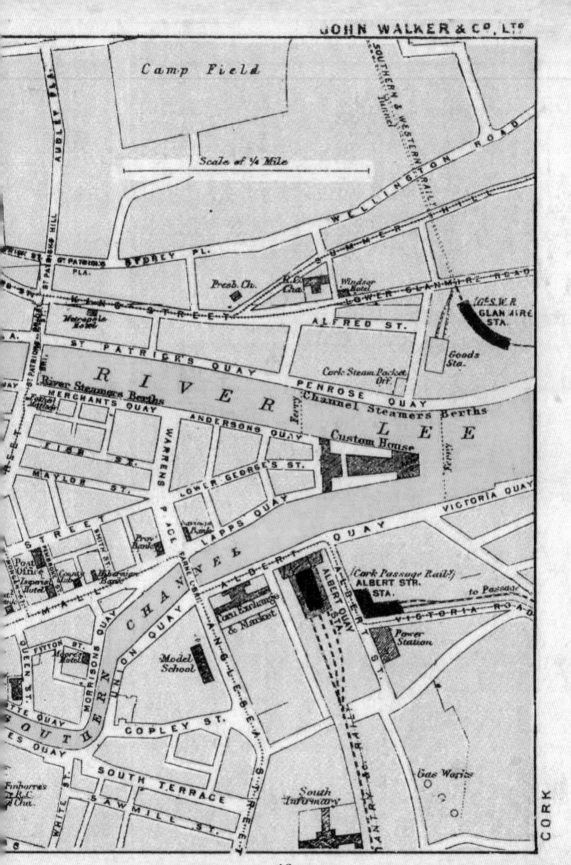

Camp Field

Scale of ¼ Mile

SOUTHERN & WESTERN RAILWAY

Tunnel

WELLINGTON ROAD

SUMMER HILL

St PATRICKS HILL

AUDLEY PLA.

ST PATRICKS PLA.

SYDNEY PL.

Presb. Ch.

R.C. Cha.

Windsor Hotel

LOWER GLANMIRE ROAD

Gt.S.W.R. GLANMIRE STA.

KING STREET

Metropole Hotel

ALFRED ST.

ST PATRICKS QUAY

Goods Sta.

R   I   V   E   R

River Steamers Berths

MERCHANTS QUAY

Father Mathew

PENROSE QUAY

Cork Steam Packet Off.

Channel Steamers Berths

ANDERSONS QUAY

L   E   E

Ferry

Custom House

Ferry

FISH ST.

MAYLOR ST.

WARRENS PLACE

LOWER GEORGE'S ST.

Custom House

VICTORIA QUAY

STREET

SMITH ST.

LAPPS QUAY

Savings Bank

VICTORIA ROAD

Prov. Banks

CHANNEL

QUAY

to Passage

Post Office

Imperial Hotel

County Club

Hibernian Bank

ALBERT QUAY

ALBERT ST.

(Cork Passage Raily)

ALBERT STR. STA.

MALL

MORRISONS QUAY

UNION QUAY

ALBERT QUAY

VICTORIA ROAD

Power Station

QUEEN ST.

FITTON ST.

Moore's Hotel

SOUTHERN

ANGLESEA ST.

Corn Exchange & Market

Model School

CHARLOTTE QUAY

ES QUAY

WHITE ST.

COPLEY ST.

S. TERRACE ST.

TERMINUS

Gas Works

Finbarre's P.R.C. Cha.

SOUTH TERRACE

SAWMILL ST.

South Infirmary

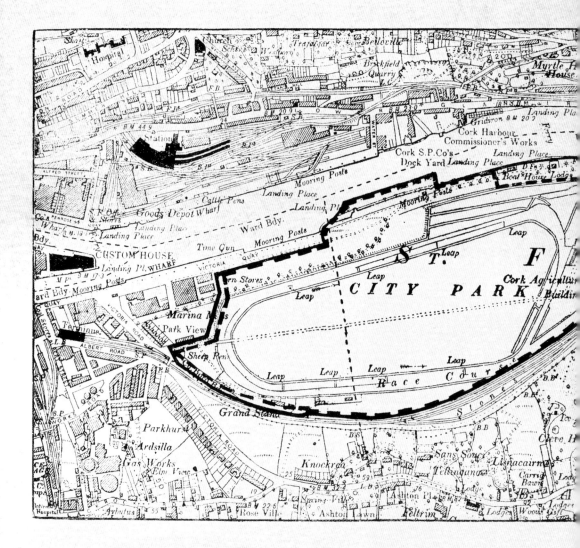

A map depicting the old Cork racecourse and the plans for Henry Ford's factory in 1917. In 1869 Sir John Arnott leased land from the Cork Corporation and established the City Park racecourse. The original corporation lease of the racecourse lands was for a term of 999 years at a ground rent of one penny per year. In May 1869 over 30,000 people attended the opening races; even King Edward VII visited the racecourse during his visit to the city in 1903.

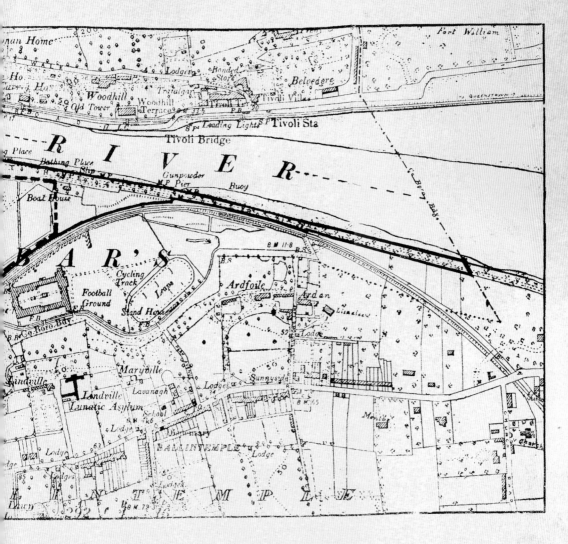

The site covered an area over 136 acres and an act of parliament had to be passed to enable Ford to buy this land. Initially the plant produced tractors and parts, which were exported all over the globe. A condition of the sale was that £200,000 was to be spent on construction and 2,000 employees were to be paid a minimum of one shilling per hour for a period of five years.

Panoramic

E arly panoramic photographs of the city are quite scarce as the photographer had to haul his cumbersome photographic equipment to the required location, but despite this, some commercial photographers such as Robert French of the firm of Lawrence, Dublin, persevered and have left us an important record of early Cork.

Previous page: A Keystone stereo view of the city from 1903, with Murphy's Brewery shaft clearly visible. The Edwardian ladies, men and children have put on their best attire for this photograph.

An Aero Films commercial postcard dating to the early 1930s. Patrick's Bridge is in the foreground and a ship is berthed beside the Railway Bridge. Many changes have taken place to the city since this aerial view was taken.

Opposite: A rare early stereo view of the city taken from Audley Place. The tentative date given on the photograph is the 1850s, but it could be earlier as Murphy's Brewery shaft is nowhere to be seen. The foreground with grazing sheep is in striking contrast to the city buildings.

This 1950s panoramic photograph was possibly taken from the heights of Shandon Church. The old buildings on Bachelor's Quay and Kyrl's Quay give this image an old-world charm. Many of these old buildings were demolished before the years of the building boom. The old wrought-iron North Gate Bridge (to the right) was still in use at this time.

An original aerial view of the north side of the city from the 1960s. The landmarks of St Mary's Cathedral, St Anne's, Shandon, and, in the foreground, Murphy's Brewery shaft ascend upwards like a ruling triumvirate. Alas, this view is no more, as the old 200-foot-high chimney shaft was demolished in 1985 – an iconic part of Cork disappeared forever.

The Cork Exhibition

ork had a tradition of holding exhibitions from as early as 1852, when the architect John Benson was commissioned to construct a massive new exhibition building, 177 feet in length and 53 feet wide. But the city's finest hour was to arrive with the opening of the Cork International Exhibition of 1902, an industrial exhibition, under the auspices of the Lord Mayor Sir Edward Fitzgerald. Such was the success of this venture that in 1903 the Greater Cork International Exhibition opened to the public. The legacy of this exhibition is Fitzgerald's Park named in honour of that Lord Mayor.

Previous page: The new purpose-built fish ponds were viewed by thousands of interested spectators. Specimens of trout, pike, perch, rudd, carp and eels could be observed. The industry hall was the largest building constructed at the exhibition, covering a massive 170,000 square feet. Most of the buildings were temporary structures constructed of timber and plaster, ensuring that they could be disassembled easily after the exhibition finished.

The water chute, located near the Industry Hall, was one of the most popular attractions. Passengers were placed in boats and were brought to the top of its seventy-foot-high pinnacle. When the boats were released down the chute, they gained momentum, swooping and skimming onto the water below at great speed.

Opposite: The Cork International Exhibition of 1902 was the ideal place to highlight new ideas and inventions. Recent advances in the scientific world were demonstrated, such as telegraphic equipment and the production of liquid gases; even a complete X-ray unit was on display. Concerts also played a major part in entertaining the crowds that flocked to the Cork Exhibition. A specially commissioned bandstand can be seen on the right of this picture.

The main concert hall could accommodate over 2,000 patrons. It also housed a great organ which was the largest ever built in the south of Ireland. It was constructed by the local firm of T. W. Magahy at the enormous cost of £1,200.

This farthing-sized token was specifically commissioned for the 1902 exhibition. In the past, Cork tokens had been used successfully to advertise businesses. Tyler's Shoe Company issued this token to advertise, 'That Tyler's Shoes are best'. Tyler's had branches at North Main Street, Patrick Street and Winthrop Street.

This photograph, taken by the local firm of Brooke Hughes, shows the refreshment rooms of the exhibition. The chalet restaurant provided afternoon teas and *table d'hôtel* dinners for the famished revellers. During the lifetime of the exhibition tens of thousands of cups of tea and coffee, and innumerable sandwiches, cakes, lunches and dinners were consumed.

John Perry & Sons were displaying their wares at stand No. 227. They were an ironmongers located at 89–91 Patrick Street. A special souvenir of their exhibition, printed by the Eagle Printing Company, South Mall, Cork, was available. This is a great example of the Celtic revival style, which was very much in vogue at this time.

By 1903 the exhibition had proved so popular that it was renamed the Greater Cork International Exhibition and several new attractions were added. The switchback railway, an early form of roller coaster, proved very popular. One contemporary advertisement claimed, 'As a nerve tonic, a down there and back on the switchback railway can be recommended'.

Every form of advertising was brought into play in order to highlight the Cork International Exhibition. A special commemorative stamp was issued featuring the arms of Cork city. From the opening day on 1 May to 1 November 1902 a staggering one and a half million people visited the grounds.

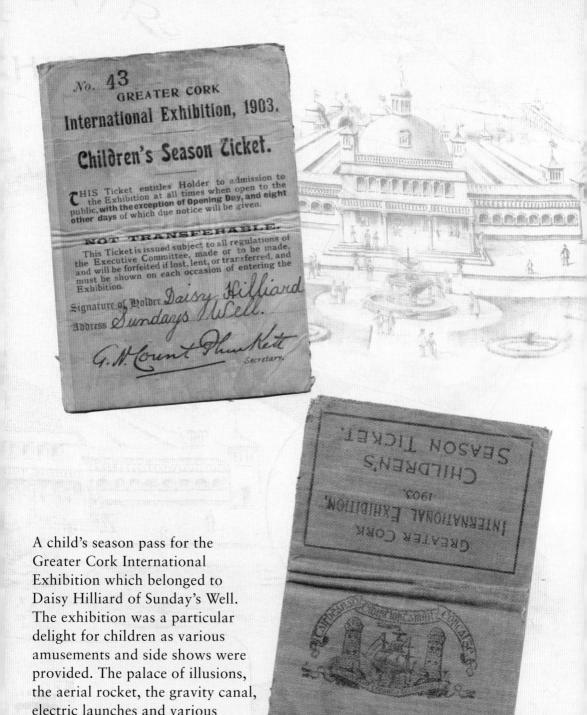

A child's season pass for the Greater Cork International Exhibition which belonged to Daisy Hilliard of Sunday's Well. The exhibition was a particular delight for children as various amusements and side shows were provided. The palace of illusions, the aerial rocket, the gravity canal, electric launches and various water sports were just some of the entertainments available.

35

Entertainment

B efore the advent of television and cinema, Cork citizens had a number of ways to entertain themselves. They could take in a show at the theatre, go for a stroll on the Mardyke or along the Marina, have a meal in one of the many impressive Cork hotels, or perhaps attend a lecture hosted by the Cork Historical and Archaeological Society and the Cork Naturalists' Field Club.

Previous page: A favourite pastime of Corkonians was a stroll down the Marina. This view dates to the early 1900s. The beautiful tree-lined avenue was an ideal place for Edwardian ladies to push their perambulators.

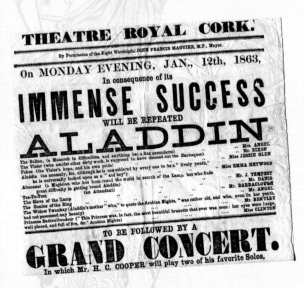

An extremely rare example of an advertising poster for the Theatre Royal. The pantomime *Aladdin* was followed by a grand concert and took place during the mayoralty of John Francis Maguire, MP, on 12 January 1863. Just months previously, in August 1862, Maguire founded *The Cork Examiner*. The site of the theatre is now occupied by the General Post Office.

A programme printed by Guy & Co. for the Cork Historical and Archaeological Society and the Cork Naturalists' Field Club for 10 March 1896. It had admission prices of one shilling and sixpence for members and two shillings for non-members and the event was held in the Imperial Hotel; evening dress was optional.

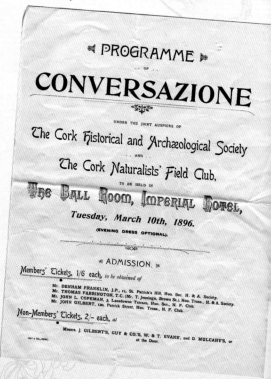

This programme was printed by Purcell & Co., Cork, for a grand concert in aid of the Blind Asylum on Infirmary Road. It was indeed a high society event with Lord Mayor Augustine Roche attending, which dates it to 1904. Lady Beatrice Pole-Carew, Lady Bandon, Lady Carbery, Lady Dobbin and Lady Hegarty were patrons.

Clarence Hall,
Imperial Hotel, Cork.

GRAND

Concert

Friday Evg., April 15th,

IN AID OF THE

Blind Asylum, Infirmary Road

UNDER THE PATRONAGE OF —

Lady Beatrice Pole-Carew
Lady Bandon
Lady Carbery
Lady Dobbin
Lady Hegarty
The Lord Mayor
(Augustine Roche, Esq., J.P.)
The High Sheriff
(Dr. Corby, T.C.)

Conductor—Herr THEO GMÜR.

PURCELL AND CO., CORK.

R. CRAIK
PIANOFORTE TUNER,
55 SOUTH MALL, CORK.

OPERA HOUSE, CORK.
Manager   Mr. JOHN HORGAN.

MONDAY, AUGUST 25th, 1902.
THE BELLE OF NEW YORK.

ASK FOR WORTHINGTON'S ALE

WORTHINGTON'S
CELEBRATED
PALE ALE

can be had at the Bars of the Theatre, and from all the leading Wine Merchants and Bottlers in the City.

Brewers by Special Appointment to
H.R.H. The Prince of Wales.

ESTABLISHED 1750.

Worthington's Ale
IS THE BEST.

AGENT—
P. J. KENNEDY, Hibernian Hotel, CORK.

WORTHINGTON'S CELEBRATED PALE ALE

Worthington & Co., Ltd.

A Cork Opera House programme dated 25 August 1902, the year of the Cork Exhibition. The show being performed was *The Belle of New York*, a musical comedy, which makes the advertisement for R. Craik, Pianoforte Tuner, rather appropriate. Worthington's pale ale was for sale in the theatre bar and was supplied by their Cork agent, P. J. Kennedy of the Hibernian Hotel.

In 1908 J. R. Bell was the manager of the Opera House and *Miss Hook of Holland* was the play being staged. The Cork firm of John Daly & Co. supplied the bottled Bass ale and Woodford Bourne's brown label whiskey could also be procured at the theatre bar.

The Pavilion Cinema, fondly known to all Corkonians as 'the Pav', first opened its doors on Thursday 10 March 1921 showing D. W. Griffith's *The Greatest Question*. This view of the cinema advertises Harold Lloyd in *For Heaven's Sake* from 1926 as the special Easter attraction. It had seating capacity for 800 people and a fine restaurant.

An Opera House programme published in aid of the rebuilding fund. A fire in 1955 had destroyed the theatre. First prize was £50, second prize was a gas cooker and third prize was a portable typewriter. The slogan 'Nearly There – Buy a Share' belies the fact that a substantial amount of money was still needed; the new building was not actually opened until 31 October 1965.

As early as 1924 Brabants were selling radios from their premises on the Grand Parade. Their slogan was 'The people who know radio'. In 1933 their most expensive radio and gramophone combination, manufactured by His Master's Voice (HMV) was selling for the princely sum of £45.

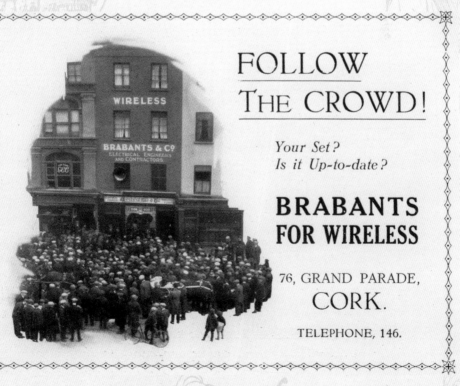

FOLLOW THE CROWD!

Your Set?
Is it Up-to-date?

BRABANTS FOR WIRELESS

76, GRAND PARADE,
CORK.

TELEPHONE, 146.

Hotel Metropole, Cork.

Finest Unlicensed Hotel in Ireland

This postcard view of the Metropole Hotel was published in 1905. Musgraves, who were staunch Methodists, owned the hotel, so it was a temperance hotel which initially did not sell alcohol. Drink was brought into the hotel only for special occasions, such as weddings. However, due to lack of trade, Musgraves were finally forced to succumb, and a bar was installed in the hotel in 1956.

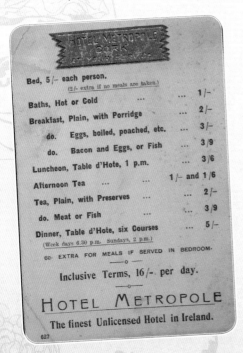

HOTEL METROPOLE CORK.

Bed, 5/- each person.
(2/- extra if no meals are taken.)

Baths, Hot or Cold	... ...	1/-
Breakfast, Plain, with Porridge	...	2/-
do. Eggs, boiled, poached, etc.	...	3/-
do. Bacon and Eggs, or Fish	...	3/9
Luncheon, Table d'Hote, 1 p.m.	...	3/6
Afternoon Tea	1/- and	1/6
Tea, Plain, with Preserves ...	...	2/-
do. Meat or Fish ...	...	3/9
Dinner, Table d'Hote, six Courses	...	5/-

(Week days 6.30 p.m. Sundays, 2 p.m.)

6d. EXTRA FOR MEALS IF SERVED IN BEDROOM.
——o——

Inclusive Terms, 16/- per day.
——o——

HOTEL METROPOLE

The finest Unlicensed Hotel in Ireland.

627

This Metropole Hotel tariff dates to 1905, a time when a room could be had for the princely sum of five shillings, or two shillings extra if meals were not purchased in the hotel. A breakfast of bacon, eggs or fish was three shillings and ninepence. A service charge of sixpence for meals in the bedrooms was applied for room service. The hotel opened its doors in 1897 and it is reputed that King Edward VII had tea there when he visited the Cork Exhibition in 1903.

A Corner of the Lounge.   Hotel Metropole, Cork.

A sketch of the Metropole's lounge.

Many large hotels such as the Metropole issued their own luggage labels, which were an ideal medium for advertising. This luggage label from the hotel dates to the time before the bar was installed and proclaims proudly that it was the finest unlicensed hotel in Ireland. Companies sent their reps to stay there, safe in the knowledge that no alcohol was available on the premises.

Royal Victoria Hotel, Cork.

A very nice Lawrence postcard of the Victoria Hotel *c.* 1900. The Victoria Hotel, Patrick Street, has played a major part in the cultural affairs of the city since its construction. It was established in 1810, making it Cork's oldest hotel. This centrally located hotel then had fifty-four rooms. Charles Dickens and Charles Stewart Parnell were just some of its famous clientele.

This Victoria Hotel luggage label dates to the 1940s, the inset vignette harking back to its busy heyday. On 27 December 1884 the second official meeting of the GAA took place there and the rules of the association were first drafted.

IMPERIAL HOTEL, CORK.

This postcard is just one of many designs that the Imperial Hotel on the South Mall used for advertising. In 1816 the Imperial Clarence Hotel was constructed at the then staggering cost of £10,000, although this included the most fashionable fixtures and fittings. The hotel was first leased to a Mr Joyce for the sum of £700 over a seven-year period. The O'Flynn group are the current owners.

A luggage label from the Imperial, showing the hotel's coat of arms. Many famous guests stayed at this hotel, including the composer Chopin, and Michael Collins spent his last night at this popular Cork institution.

The Imperial issued this card in the 1950s to allow intended guests to reserve accommodation. Early arrival was advised as rooms could not be held later than 8.30 p.m. unless prior notice was given. The Imperial had eighty-one rooms.

SPECIAL TO ORDER

Roast Chicken & Bacon   ... 3/-

LUNCHEON
12.30 - 3 p.m
2/6d

Clear Vermicelli
or
Cream of Celery

Chicken & Ham Cutlets
or
Stewed Steak & Carrots
or
Grilled Sausages. Mashed Potatoes
or
Roast Leg of Mutton
or
Roast Sirloin of Beef
Cabbage. Mashed Turnips. Spinach
Boiled. Mashed. Baked Potatoes

Apple Fritters
or
Rice Pudding
or
Jelly or Trifle or Carrageen
or
Stewed Figs
or
Vanilla Cream or Vanilla Ice

COFFEE

A rare survivor, this menu from the Savoy cinema and restaurant dates to 3 March 1943. The menu gives us a fascinating glimpse into a dining experience in Cork during the Second World War when it was illegal to serve butter with lunches or dinners due to strict rationing. The meals appear quite bland, although chicken and sirloin of beef were both available.

The Cork Operatic Society held their play *A Country Girl* at the Father Mathew Hall in 1956.

VIEW OF INTERIOR OF 71 & 72, PATRICK STREET, CORK.

Hot and Cold Luncheons and Light Refreshments.

Ices, Afternoon Tea Cakes, Chocolate and Bon-Bons.

F. H. THOMPSON & SON, LTD., PATRICK STREET. CORK.

71 & 72

FACTORY—King Street, CORK.   BRANCHES—Bridge Street, CORK;

An advertisement for the very popular confectioners F. H. Thompson, whose bakery was located on MacCurtain Street. They also had a series of restaurants in the city centre at Patrick Street, Bridge Street and Princes Street. Afternoon teas were a particular favourite with the ladies. A bewildering array of cakes, teas and ice cream was available to the Cork public. Thompson's finally closed its doors in 1984.

The Lottery was a favourite with ordinary folk and gamblers alike from the time of its inception. This Cork advertisement from 1799 declares that there were twenty-seven capital prizes available for the Lottery. The Cork agent was the printer James Haly at Castle Street and by 1803 the Cork Lottery office had handled £380,000 in tickets and prizes.

LOSE NO TIME.

27 *Capital Prizes*

Are in the IRISH LOTTERY to be drawn on 23d July next,

THE TICKETS AND SHARES

Of which are now on Sale at the

Old Hibernian Office,

NO. 12, CAPEL-STREET, DUBLIN.

The Character the above Office has maintained for 19 Years will, BROWNE presumes, establish for his SHARES a decided preference.

TICKET BUYERS

in the City of Cork, and its Vicinity, are respectfully acquainted that TICKETS and SHARES, from BROWNE's Office, can be had at

MR. JAMES HALY's,

KING'S-ARMS, EXCHANGE, CORK,

At the most reduced Prices.

TO BE SOLD BY AUCTION,

A private photograph taken at the time of the 1902 Cork Exhibition. This exclusive play was held in the gardens of one of the large private houses at Sunday's Well. It shows the two main performers, Judy Wells and Albert Short, taking a bow in front of an appreciative audience.

Rowing on the River Lee was a very popular sport in the early 1900s, as it still is today. Photographed by the Cork photographer Brooke Hughes, these Shandon Boat Club members clearly demonstrate the popularity of the sport. No fewer than forty-one gentlemen feature in their very smart attire.

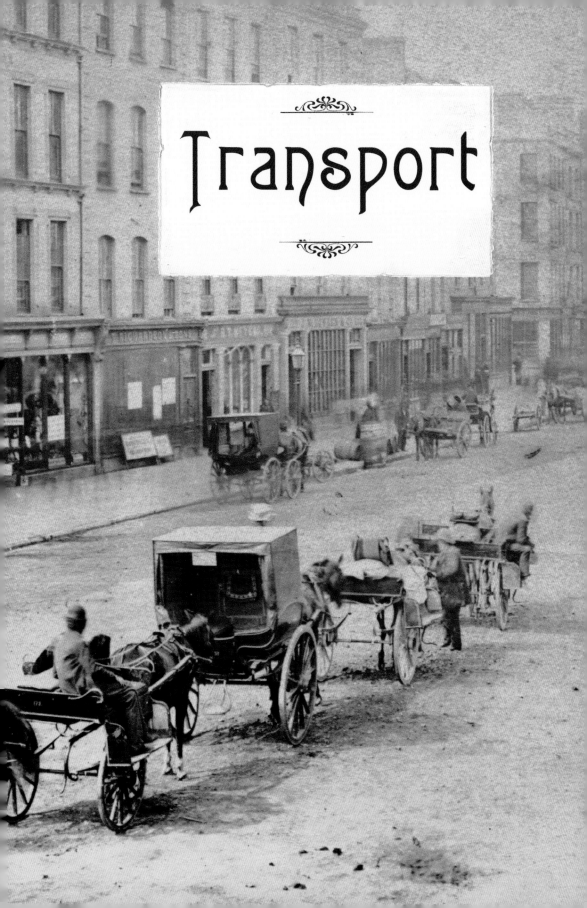

Transport

Horse-drawn Vehicles

Prior to the advent of the electric tram and the motor car, horse-drawn vehicles were the main mode of transport. In 1810 the firm of James Johnson established his carriage works at Nelson Place (now Emmet Place). By 1867 the firm of Robert Julian, South Mall, was advertising broughams, barouches, wagonettes and every variety of fashionable carriages. Guy's Munster Directory of 1893 lists no less than eleven coach builders in the city.

Previous page: An early stereo view of Patrick Street, *c.* 1891, when the street divide was dictated by the line of hackney cars which were parked in the centre of the street. This street scene includes various horses and carts of all descriptions carrying their goods.

Hackneys awaiting passengers at Patrick Street in 1895, with various businesses in the background boldly advertising their products. The entrance to Drawbridge Street is just beside No. 118, McTaggart's Cycle Depot.

The Grand Parade was another designated hackney stop, and muddy streets were the order of the day. To the right, the religious Tract Book Society was pedalling its wares, which consisted solely of protestant literature.

A stereo view of Bridge Street, 1891, before mechanised transport. This street was quite a busy thoroughfare as it was adjacent to Patrick's Bridge. Commercial premises such as confectioners, vintners, tobacconists, grocers and printers all sold their wares there.

This ornate hand-coloured glass lantern slide dates to *c*. 1890. Beautiful iron railings adorn the Berwick fountain, erected in 1860 by Judge Walter Berwick. A local ditty about the fountain went as follows:

Judge Berwick – God bless him! Ah, how could he tell
The five hundred he gave would give us such a sell;
For before it was finished, twelve hundred it cost
But mavorne! All the labour and money was lost.

The jingle was a type of horse-drawn hackney peculiar to Cork. It was a lightweight vehicle, ideal for traversing the steep hills of the city whilst keeping the enclosed passengers safe from the elements.

Campao ó Concaiġ.
CORK JINGLE.

The top of Patrick Street with the Standard Watch Company's premises visible across the bridge. This photograph can be accurately dated, as the company premises only existed for six months and never reopened after a disastrous fire in 1895. The premises was replaced by the new turreted building after this older building was destroyed by the fire.

Trams and Buses

From Cork's first horse-drawn trams, which lasted a mere three years (1872–1875), to the heyday of the electric tramway, Cork's citizens had a love affair with trams. Unfortunately their demise was hastened by the arrival of buses competing for their business in 1926. Buses, unlike trams, were not constrained by fixed routes and they were also far quicker than their slower-moving counterparts. Because of this the end of the electric trams came on 30 September 1931. One of the fine original pictures featured in this section was taken just two weeks prior to their sad demise.

The first of the horse-drawn trams appeared in Patrick Street in 1872. One piece of doggerel records: 'As I was going down Patrick's Street, I heard a lady say: "Oh it's jolly to be riding, On the new tramway".' By 1875 the horse-drawn tramway system had proved to be a failure, due to its limited routes, and the rails were removed in 1876.

The palates of Cork's rich public were treated to Gilbey's Rubicon Australian burgundy at two shillings per bottle when this photograph was taken. The route of this 1920s tram was Summerhill to Sunday's Well. The lady on the right had a very good viewpoint as the tram made its way along its route.

An original Cork Electric Tramways and Lighting Company ticket on which the various routes are printed. Singer's corner was a particularly busy tram terminus, but this ticket was punched Summerhill to Grand Parade and the fare was a penny.

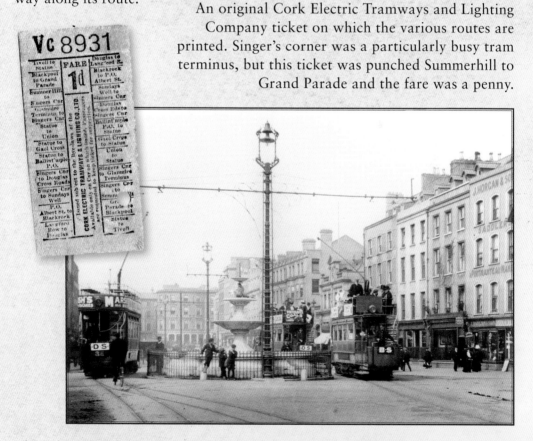

This photograph shows a very busy tram scene at the Grand Parade around 1900. Note the beautiful wrought-iron railings which protected the Berwick fountain. This tram pole held the largest amount of electric cable in the city for the tramway system.

This image can be dated to 1900–1 as Morgan Street was only used for a short time as a loop to enter the South Mall. Morgan Street was extremely narrow, about twelve feet in width, and the trams caused severe disruption to other traffic trying to use it. One of the trams is advertising high-class coals from the Cork Steam Packet Company.

A stereo view of an electric tram outside Lester's Chemists, 107 Patrick Street. The destination board on the side of the tram reads 'To Exhibition', indicating that it would take its passengers to the Cork Exhibition of 1902–3. This tram travelled up Washington Street onto the Western Road as far as Wellington Bridge (Thomas Davis Bridge).

It was a rare event to have so many trams lined up outside the Patrick Street terminus. This photograph was probably taken when the tramway men went en masse to the North Cathedral to pray for Lord Mayor Terence MacSwiney, who was on hunger strike in Brixton prison in 1920. MacSwiney died on 25 October 1920.

This amended Cork Electric Tramways regulations and bye-laws schedule for 1910 stipulated that every electric tram should be fitted with a speedometer so the driver was aware of his vehicle's speed. Emergency brake blocks were to be fitted, as well as an electric brake. A warning bell was to be sounded to enable adequate warning of its arrival to pedestrians and other traffic.

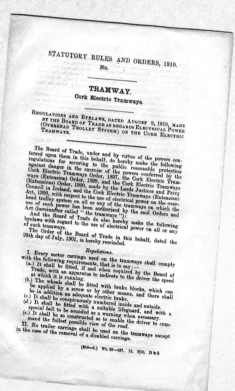

PARNELL BRIDGE. CORK. 1942. W. L.

The problems encountered erecting cables and tram standards on this swivel bridge must have been quite challenging for the Cork Tramways Company. The magnificent limestone architecture of the old Provincial Bank and the Cork Savings Bank provides a beautiful backdrop to this image.

ork City, Ireland

This picture was taken by one of the crew of the destroyer USS *Whipple* on a visit to Cork in 1927. The Douglas–Blackpool tram is advertising Gill & Co. tea blenders, who also sold cakes and jams at No. 18 Princes Street. The ornate windows of the Central Stores provided a picturesque background to the nearby tram stop. Three jarveys to the right are clearly enjoying a chat after their day's work.

This press photograph was taken just two weeks before the closure of the tramway system in Cork. The three main systems of transport in the city are shown here: a tram, a hackney and the new arrival, a bus operated by the Irish Omnibus Company. The end for the electric trams finally came on 30 September 1931 amidst the noise of foghorns and a brilliant firework display.

This photograph of a CIE bus was taken outside the old Woolworth's shop on Patrick Street. It dates from the early 1940s, during the Second World War. Note the starting handle hanging below the radiator of the bus. This primitive starting device was in use before the age of the electric starter motor. Brains as well as brawn were required to breathe life into these massive engines, as the starting device could be temperamental!

St. Patrick Street, Cork.

Trams and buses are vying for passengers in this commercial postcard, which dates to 1926. The Cork Motor Services Company was then utilising Daimler open-top double-decker buses. Competition from bus companies was to bring a swift end to the trams just five years later.

This photograph is of a very busy Patrick Street scene. The double-decker bus in the centre was part of Cork's transport system six years prior to their introduction in Dublin. Leyland single-decker buses could seat 32 passengers, whilst the Leyland Titan could seat 51 passengers comfortably. The old busmen's hut, a feature in the middle of the street for decades, is now sadly gone.

Great Southern Railways (Omnibus Department)

CORK CITY SERVICES

Alterations in Timetable from 27th April, 1942

SUNDAY'S WELL/BISHOPSTOWN

Week-days—Half-hourly service from 8.0 a.m to 10.0 p.m. First cars from termini 8.0 a.m.

Sundays—Half-hourly service from 10.0 a.m. to 1.30 p.m.; 3.15 p.m. to 5.0 p.m.; 6.45 p.m to 8 30 p.m

STATUE/MAYFIELD

Week-days—Half-hourly service from 7.50 a.m. to 8.35 a.m.; 9.35 a.m. to 11.35 a.m.; 2.5 p.m. to 5.35 p.m. and 6.35 p.m. to 10 p.m.

Quarter-hourly service from 8 35 a.m. to 9.35 a.m. 11.35 a.m. to 2.5 p.m.; 5.35 p.m. to 6.35 p.m. First car from Mayfield 7.50 a.m.

Sundays—Half-hourly service from 10.0 a.m. to 1.30 p.m.; 3.0 to 5.0 p.m.; 6 30 p.m. to 8.30 p.m.

COLLEGE ROAD/SUNDAY'S WELL This service will be operated in future between College Rd and Statue only.

Week-days—Half-hourly service from 7.45 a.m. to 10.0 p.m. First car from Statue 8.0 a.m and from College Road 7.45 a.m.

Sundays—Half-hourly service from 10.0 a.m. to 1.30 p.m.; 3.0 p.m. to 5 p.m.; 6.30 p.m to 8.30 p.m.

STATUE/POULADUFF Service as at present

STATUE/BLACKROCK

Week-days—18 minutes service from 7.30 a.m. to 8.30 a.m.; 10.40 a.m. to 11.50 a.m.; 3.18 p.m. to 4.30 p.m.; 6.54 p.m. to 10.0 p.m.

Nine Minutes service from 8.30 a.m. to 10.40 a.m., 11.50 a.m. to 3.18 p.m.; 4.30 p.m. to 6.54 p.m. First car from Blackrock 7.30 a.m. and from Statue 7.30 a.m.

Sundays—12 minutes service from 10.0 a.m. to 1.30 p.m.; 3.0 p.m' to 5.0 p.m.; 6.30 p.m. to 8.30 p.m.

MAGAZINE ROAD/TIVOLI

Week-days—20 minutes service from 7.30 a.m. to 10.0 p.m. First service car from Magazine Rd 7 30 a.m. and Tivoli 7.30 a.m.

Sundays—20 minutes service from 9.50 a.m. to 1.30 p.m.; 3.0 p.m. to 5.0 p.m. and 6.30 p.m. to 8.30 p.m.

TURNER'S CROSS/GURRANEBRAHER

Week-days—Quarter-hourly service from 7.33 a.m. to 10.0 p.m. First car from Turner's Cross 7.33 a.m. and Gurranebraher 7.40 a.m.

Saturdays—12 minutes service will be operated.

Sundays—Quarter-hourly service from 10.0 a.m. to 1.30 p.m.; 3.0 p.m. to 5.0 p.m. and 6.30 p.m. to 8.30 p.m.

DOUGLAS/SPANGLE HILL/BLACKPOOL

Week-days—12 minutes service from 7.30 a.m. to 7.0 p.m. 15 minutes service from 7.0 p.m. to 10.0 p.m First car from Douglas 7.30 a.m., Blackpool 7.36 a.m. and Spangle Hill 7.48 a.m.

Sundays—12 minutes service from 10.0 a.m to 1.30 p.m.; 3.0 p.m. to 5.0 p.m. and 6.30 p.m. to 8.30 p.m.

DILLON'S CROSS/WILTON/FARNALEA PARK

Week-days—10 minutes service from 8.0 a.m. to 3.20 p.m.; 5.0 p.m. to 7.0 p.m. 20 minutes service from 3.20 p.m. to 5.0 p.m. and 7.0 p.m. to 10.0 p.m. First bus from Dillon's Cross 8.0 a.m., Wilton 8.15 a.m. Farnalea Park 8.5 a.m.

Sundays—12 minutes service from 10.0 a.m. to 1.30 p.m. 3.0 p.m. to 5.0 p.m.; 6.30 p.m. to 8.30 p.m.

STATUE/FORD'S & DUNLOP'S FACTORY
Service as at present

STATUE/SUNBEAM FACTORY
Service as at present

Last car from Statue to all termini will leave at **10 p.m. Week-days** and **8.30 p.m. Sundays**

Full particulars can be obtained from Conductors; Company's Depot, 40/41 Grand Parade, Statue Hut, or on application to the Manager, Omnibus Department, Transport House, Dublin.

Kingsbridge Station,
22nd April, 1942

By Order,
GENERAL MANAGER.

HOUSTON. PRINTER, CORK

In 1942 the Great Southern Railways Omnibus Department issued this amended travel timetable due to fuel shortages. Buses were provided to bring the workers employed in Ford's, Dunlop's and the Sunbeam factory to their workplaces. The last bus left from the statue at 10 p.m. on weekdays and 8.30 p.m. on Sundays.

Railways and Locomotives

Cork had some marvellous railway companies. The Cork, Bandon & South Coast Railway opened for rail traffic in 1851. Over time this railway network extended to the towns of Bandon, Clonakilty, Dunmanway, Skibbereen and Bantry. There was also the Cork, Blackrock & Passage Railway which serviced as far as Crosshaven, while the Cork & Muskerry Light Railway, affectionately known as the hook and eye, travelled along the Western Road to Blarney. These railway companies had wonderful locomotives, many of which were given names, such as the *City of Cork*, *Blarney*, *Peake*, *Donoughmore* and *Dripsey*.

This scene at the Cork Glanmire station is of locomotive No. 312 and the Rosslare boat train. Locomotive No. 312, a Great Southern & Western Coey Class 309, was built at Neilson, Reid & Co. Ltd, Scotland, in 1903.

This locomotive named *Pike* was built for the Cork & Youghal Railway, which had its own engines built between 1859–62. In 1876 this line was absorbed into the Great Southern & Western Railway.

A CIE diesel locomotive heading towards Alfred Street with a guard's wagon attached. This photograph from the late 1960s was taken at a time when trains still traversed the city's two railway bridges amidst traffic.
Courtesy of the Walter McGrath collection

One of the Cork & Muskerry Light Railway carriages at its terminus in Bishop's Marsh (now the River Lee Hotel). St Finbarre's Cathedral to the extreme left peers through, revealing its location. This railway survived until 29 December 1934 when the last train left the Western Road for Blarney.

1914.

THE

Silvery :: :: River Lee.

CORK, BLACKROCK & PASSAGE RAILWAY COMPANY

Cork Harbour ::
AND :: ::
Atlantic Ocean.

GRAND

DAILY EXCURSION

(Saturdays Excepted)

From CORK (St. Patrick's Bridge)

Months of July and August, and Sundays June and September

INCLUDING

Luncheon at the Crosshaven Hotel,

BY THE

Cork, Blackrock & Passage Railway Co.'s

STEAMERS and TRAINS.

FARES—First Class, 3/6; Third Class, 3/-

Purcell & Co., Cork.

In 1914 the Cork, Blackrock & Passage Railway Company organised a grand daily excursion from Cork city for the months of June, July, August and September. The Crosshaven Hotel was the venue for luncheon upon arrival. First-class passengers paid three shillings and sixpence whilst the third-class carriage passengers paid three shillings.

The general regulations for the Cork & Muskerry Light Railway for 1912 give an example of the diverse goods carried: motor cycles, horses, cattle, butter and other small packages were transported to and from the city by this light railway. One macabre entry records the charges involved in conveying a corpse – sixpence per mile for an adult, while a child's corpse cost fourpence a mile. If the deceased had died because of an infectious disease the remains had to be enclosed in a leaden coffin.

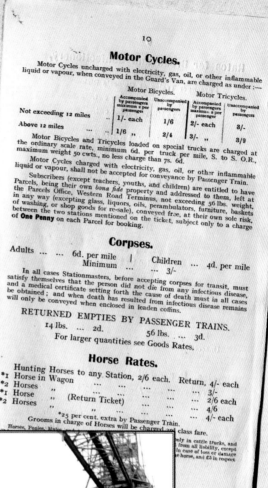

Motor Cycles.

Motor Cycles uncharged with electricity, gas, oil, or other inflammable liquid or vapour, when conveyed in the Guard's Van, are charged as under :—

	Motor Bicycles.		Motor Tricycles.	
	Accompanied by passengers maximum 2 per passenger	Unaccompanied by passengers	Accompanied by passengers maximum 2 per passenger	Unaccompanied by passengers
Not exceeding 12 miles	1/- each	1/6	2/- each	3/-
Above 12 miles	1/6 ,,	2/4	3/- ,,	3/9

Motor Bicycles and Tricycles loaded on special trucks are charged at the ordinary scale rate, minimum 6d. per truck per mile, S. to S. O.R., maximum weight 50 cwts., no less charge than 7s. 6d.

Motor Cycles charged with electricity, gas, oil, or other inflammable liquid or vapour, shall not be accepted for conveyance by Passenger Train.

Subscribers (except teachers, youths, and children) are entitled to have Parcels, being their own bona fide property and addressed to them, left at the Parcels Office, Western Road Terminus, not exceeding 56 lbs. weight, in any way (excepting glass, liquors, oils, perambulators, furniture, baskets of washing, or shop goods for re-sale), conveyed free, at their own sole risk, between the two stations mentioned on the ticket, subject only to a charge of **One Penny** on each Parcel for booking.

Corpses.

Adults	6d. per mile	Children	4d. per mile
Minimum			3/-

In all cases Stationmasters, before accepting corpses for transit, must satisfy themselves that the person did not die from any infectious disease, and a medical certificate setting forth the cause of death must in all cases be obtained ; and when death has resulted from infectious disease remains will only be conveyed when enclosed in leaden coffins.

RETURNED EMPTIES BY PASSENGER TRAINS.

14 lbs.	2d.	56 lbs.	3d.

For larger quantities see Goods Rates.

Horse Rates.

Hunting Horses to any Station, 2/6 each. Return, 4/- each

*1 Horse in Wagon					2/6 each
*2 Horses ,,					3/-
*1 Horse ,, (Return Ticket)					2/6 each
*2 Horses ,,					4/6
					4/- each

*25 per cent. extra by Passenger Train.

Grooms in charge of Horses will be charged 3rd class fare.

Horses, Ponies, Mules ... only in cattle trucks, and
... from all liability, except
... In case of loss or damage
e horse, and £5 in respect

Two Ford workers look at the ingenious system created on the roof to transport coal efficiently to all parts of the factory. The hopper was loaded with coal, which was then discharged onto the wagons which had hinged floors. A lever was pulled when the small locomotive reached its destination releasing the coal directly to where it was required in the factory below.

This photograph was taken by an amateur photographer at Glanmire railway station in 1919. He used a half plate camera to take this image of locomotive No. 329, which was built at Inchicore, Dublin.

F. 74
5000—4-04.

Cork, Bandon & South Coast Railway.

B'NEEN & E'KEANE

A very rare survivor: a luggage label which was issued by the Cork, Bandon & South Coast Railway. The luggage that this label was attached to was destined for Ballineen and Enniskeane in West Cork, where the railway had stations.

Right: Some of the larger railway companies, such as the Cork, Bandon & South Coast Railway issued their own green 2d stamps. The Cork & Macroom Direct Railway did likewise with a blue 2d stamp. Both of these railways operated from the city, sending parcels by the railway network.

The main modes of Cork
transport on the Western
Road in the late 1920s.

BLARNEY TRAIN, WESTERN ROAD, CORK.

Motor Cars

G uy's directory for 1904 lists three motor garages in the city. The firms of Robert Julian of 12 South Mall and James Johnson of Nelson Place were formerly carriage builders that now turned their attention to servicing horseless carriages for their new-found clientele. By the 1930s the taxi firm of Denis O'Connor, Hardwick Street, used Rolls Royce and Daimler cars to convey its customers.

This advertisement for Denis O'Connor from the 1930s, clearly shows that the affluent citizens of Cork could be chauffeured about in style.

A hackney driver is unperturbed as he is passed by this new-fangled form of transport whizzing its way down Patrick Street. With the arrival of the Cork Electric Tram Co. in 1898, horse-drawn transport had become accustomed to mechanised vehicles on the roads.

This Bridge Street image dates to the early days of the motor car, *c.* 1910. The street catered for two-way traffic at this time. A large motor car making its way towards Patrick Street would have been a rare sight. The occupants of the car appear to be dressed in their finery.

A rare survivor: a copy of *The Ford Times* issued by Henry Ford & Son in January 1939. Just months later the Second World War erupted, but production continued. By 1942 no raw materials were available for car production. Some strange items were made: wooden clogs, screwdrivers, even carriages for Bren guns for the Irish army. Nails from packing crates were straightened and timber salvaged by Ford employees – whatever was necessary to keep the plant open.

SUPPLEMENTARY
REGULATIONS
FOR THE

CORK MOTOR RACE

TO BE HELD ON THE

CARRIGROHANE CIRCUIT

NEAR CORK CITY

On SATURDAY, 16th MAY, 1936

UNDER THE INTERNATIONAL SPORTING CODE,
NATIONAL COMPETITION RULES OF THE ROYAL
IRISH AUTOMOBILE CLUB, RACING RULES OF
THE IRISH MOTOR RACING CLUB LIMITED,
AND THESE SUPPLEMENTARY REGULATIONS

STEWARDS OF THE MEETING:
P. S. BRADY, Esq., The Irish Motor Racing Club Limited.
W. H. FREEMAN, Esq., The Irish Motor Racing Club Limited.
STAMFORD H. ROCHE, Esq., P.C., Royal Irish Automobile Club.
CAPTAIN W. J. THOMPSON, Ulster Automobile Club.

CLERK OF THE COURSE:
MAJOR NIALL MacNEILL.

SECRETARY OF THE MEETING:
D. J. SCANNELL.

This race is approved for trade participation by the Society of Motor Manufacturers and Traders and the Society of Irish Motor Traders, and is open to Irish,
English, Scottish and Welsh entrants and drivers.

PROMOTED BY

THE IRISH MOTOR RACING CLUB LTD.,

1, Cavendish Row, Dublin.

(TELEPHONE NO. DUBLIN 44264).

to whom all correspondence on the subject of entry and
participation should be addressed

WITH THE CO-OPERATION OF

THE CORK MOTOR RACE COMMITTEE,

Imperial Hotel, Cork.

LANDONS, PRINTERS, CORK.

Lord Mayor Seán French promoted Cork's first major motor race and the Carrigrohane Road was the ideal location. A total of 27 cars entered and the prize fund totalled £650, a significant amount. The winner was R. E. Tongue whose average speed was 85.53 mph in a 1488cc ERA car.

Cork Airport

The selection of photographs included here were taken by Mr Peter Dooley just a few short months after Cork airport opened for business. Initially the two airline companies that operated from the airport were Aer Lingus, which flew Viscount aeroplanes, and Cambrian Airways (later taken over by British Airways), which flew Dakota DC 3s.

The first plane to land on a commercial flight at Cork airport on Monday 16 October 1961 was an Aer Lingus Viscount similar to the one pictured here. There were six flights, both inward and outward, on opening day. It was expected that over 30,000 passengers would travel through the airport during its first year of operation. An Aer Lingus flight to London cost £17 7s return and the special excursion rate was £15 6s. Jacobs & Company chartered the first official passenger flight to Dublin.

A lone Cambrian Airways Dakota DC 3 at Cork airport in the early days of its operation. Aer Lingus and Cambrian both published notices in the newspapers advertising that 'Cork is only minutes away from the main British cities'. During the winter schedule for 1962 the airport did not open on Sundays.

Aer Lingus personnel on standby, ready to attend to a Viscount which had just landed at Cork airport in 1962. The airport had cost in excess of one million pounds to build, an enormous sum of money in those days.

Industry

During its history, Cork has had many fine industries, including textile manufacturing, brewing, bacon processing and car manufacturing. Many of the most famous of these, including Henry Ford and Dwyer & Company, have now sadly disappeared from the Cork landscape, but their memory is preserved in images of their workers, products and factories.

Previous page: My father, Denis Lenihan, and Tucker Lyons on a horse and dray in 1942. Murphy's Brewery, in common with many Cork firms, had their own horses and stables before the advent of lorries. The old wooden barrels, tierces and hogsheads were replaced with the new steel barrels, which were then known as iron lungs.

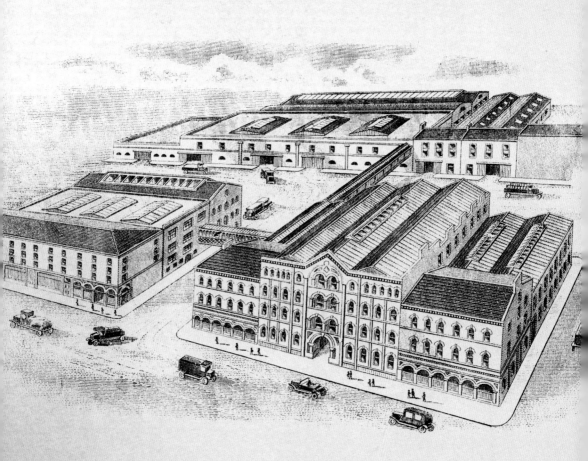

The Founder

Chairman &
Managing Director
1889 – 1902

Chairman &
Managing Director
1902 – 1925

James Dwyer
Born   Died
1844 – 1902

Walter Dwyer
Born   Died
1851 – 1925

James Dwyer 1798–1889

The sketch of Dwyer & Company (*opposite*) gives some indication of the sheer scale of their operation. It extended from Washington Street to Hanover Street, all part of their massive industrial empire. Some of the buildings were joined by long tunnels, which added to their capacity. Dwyers' main warehouse was situated at Nos 24–29 Washington Street. The main drapery department sold shirts, woollens, dresses, hats and ready-to-wear clothing. Fancy goods, china, stationary, hardware, toys and groceries were also stocked.

Dwyer & Company established different industries, such as the Lee Hosiery Company, which was part of their garment-making department. This picture shows some of their female employees working away busily at their sewing machines. Most of this work was paid by the system of piece-work – the more you produced the more you were paid. Woe betide you if your machine broke, as this meant you were paid nothing.

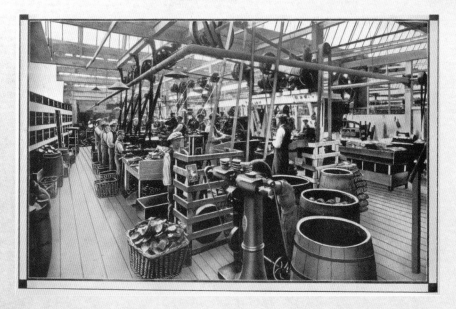

Another important manufacturing arm of the Dwyer operation was the Lee Boot Company. Various styles of shoes were produced and such was the quality that thousands of pairs of shoes were exported to Britain and further afield.

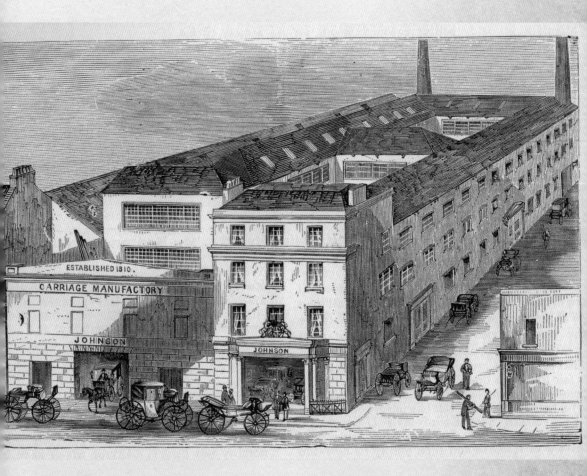

The firm of James Johnson, established in 1810, was one of the largest carriage manufacturers in the south of Ireland. In 1892 it employed upwards of seventy men at its premises in Nelson Place (now Emmet Place). The latest machinery designed by Mr Johnson could produce fifty wheel spokes in one hour. In later years Johnson & Perrott became well established motor dealers and continue to trade to this day.

The old cranes located to the rear of Henry Ford's were ideal for loading and discharging automotive parts and cars onto the ships berthed at the wharf adjoining the factory. The Ford factory opened in 1917. My grandfather drove one of these cranes before he emigrated to Dagenham. Unfortunately in the early 1980s they were dismantled, as during a severe storm the cranes propelled down their rails and damaged many new cars. The factory itself closed in 1984.

This 1936 photograph shows Ford cars ready for shipment. Ford's was trading under the Fordson name at this time. The old Henry Ford maxim was 'you can have any colour you like once it's black'. Apparently black paint dried much quicker than the other colours, enabling a much quicker rate of production.

This is an early Ford advertisement for a light van, weighing in at nearly a ton and costing £165 ex-works. Judging by the crude aerodynamics of this four-wheeled monster it was certainly not built for speed. The latest technological advances in windscreen technology were used in the form of non-splintering glass. One can only marvel at what the fuel consumption figures might have been.

This Henry Ford advertisement, which dates from the 1960s, displays the latest in automobile comfort, the Zephyr Mark IV, offering a choice of V2 engines and power-assisted brakes unrivalled in its class. The Zephyr had a bench seat which enabled three people to sit up front. The gear changer was on the steering wheel column, unlike standard transmissions.

The Zephyr's comprehensive specification includes many technical innovations and luxury features. It has four wheel independent suspension and power-assisted disc brakes, a choice of two very advanced V engines, and Ford's exclusive Aeroflow ventilation system. The car's interior is extremely spacious. A full width front bench seat and convex side windows enable six adults to travel in comfort. Above all, there is, in the Zephyr Mark IV, the degree of finish and attention to detail which is appropriate to a car of distinction.

The magnificent, iconic advertising trademark of James J. Murphy & Co. Ltd. Eugene Sandow, the 1891 world weight-lifting champion, endorsed Murphy's famous stout and porter forty years before Guinness used a similar form of advertising.

A photograph of Murphy's Brewery city store in 1957. It is unusual that the Ford truck is loaded with wooden barrels whilst the horse and dray has the new-fangled steel barrels. To the left is Denis O'Mahony and in the background Denis Lenihan and Mickey Murphy. The horse's name was Paddy and he was a particular favourite with the brewery workers.

A 1930 photograph of Tim O'Sullivan inspecting barrels on this Murphy's truck. This was a particularly poor time for the brewery due to a continuing slump in agricultural prices and less demand for its products. By 1931 the brewery was producing a mere 30,000 barrels of stout, a small percentage of its capability.

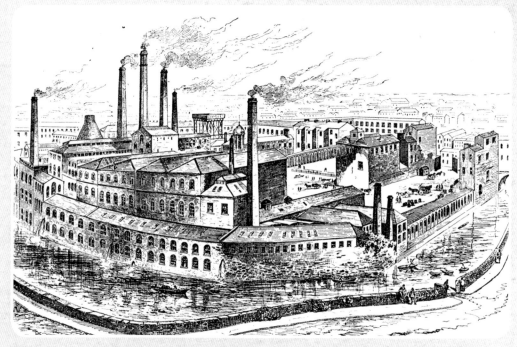

The Beamish & Crawford Brewery in all its glory. Nine chimney stacks were in use demonstrating the size of this mammoth brewing concern. As early as 1667 a brew house was located on the site of Beamish & Crawford and the history of brewing on this site could date back to medieval times. In 1791 William Beamish and William Crawford purchased Edward Allen's Brewery and Beamish & Crawford traded as the Cork Porter Brewery. By the early 1830s it was the largest brewery in Ireland. In its heyday the brewery accounted for 12 per cent of all the rates collected in the city. By the 1860s the site covered an area well in excess of four acres. Unfortunately, Beamish & Crawford is now closed, but Beamish stout is still brewed by Heineken Ireland and it continues to be a favourite tipple with Cork stout drinkers.

A CORNER OF THE BOARD ROOM

CARVING AND DECORATION BY BREWERY WORKMEN

On the shelf are two old glass wine bottles dated 1708

Sir John Arnott purchased Abbot's Brewery in 1861 and renamed it St Finbarre's Brewery on account of its close proximity to St Finbarre's Cathedral. This image is from a poster printed by Guy's printers and it is an extremely rare view of Arnott's brewery. It was situated in an ideal location near the River Lee and the Cork & Muskerry Light Railway. In 1906 the brewery was demolished to make way for the building of the Sharman Crawford Technical School.

The English Market has been part of Cork's history and culture since 1788. This postcard view of M. & E. Sheehan, located within the market, proudly displaying their fish, dates to the early twentieth century. This business closed in 2000.

The Cork Furniture Stores was the precursor to the very popular Roches Stores. This illustration is taken from its 1913 catalogue and shows its premises at Merchant Street. The prosperity of the company was mainly due to extremely low overheads, which enabled the selling of goods at up to 25 per cent cheaper than their rivals.

An unusual drawing of the old Lunham Brothers bacon factory at Kemp Street, with a plan of the building in the bottom right corner. This building was designed by the Cork architect Robert Walker. Due to the sheer size and mechanisation of the plant, tens of thousands of pigs were slaughtered and processed annually.

The Hive Iron Works was the largest foundry in the city and was established by Thomas Addison Barnes in 1800. In 1813 Richard Perrott became a partner in the firm, which was located in Hanover Street. This original Hive Iron Works plaque bears Perrott's name, as by the 1830s he was the sole proprietor. Many examples of the company's railings, gates, bollards and manhole covers still survive in the city today.

Banknotes
and Tokens

ork, in common with other parts of Ireland, had its share of private banks. Leslie's, Cotter & Kellett's and Roche's, to name but a few, issued their own banknotes, some of which are reproduced here. Cork coinage such as copper tokens, medallions and a rare Cork penny dated 1659 are just some of the items included, as well as the only official banknote featuring St Patrick's Bridge and its surrounds, shown here. The reverse of a £5 ploughman note, this is the only official banknote to feature a scene of Cork city. St Anne's, Shandon, and St Mary's, Pope's Quay, are depicted. The hills in the background give no hint of the development that was to follow the building of Cathedral Road and Gurranabraher in the 1930s.

Private banks issued promissory banknotes such as this example, which were then realised at face value. This note, from Leslie's Bank, was valued at one pound and five shillings.

The banknotes in this section are from a private collection.

The private bank of Stephen and James Roche issued this Cork banknote for one guinea on 18 December 1817. The note could only be redeemed at the bank between the hours of 10 a.m. and 2 p.m.

This banknote from the private bank of Cotter & Kellett is a rare survivor and its value was thirty shillings. These notes were redeemed in Irish currency, as sterling had a higher value.

This three guinea note, which amounted to three pounds three shillings, was made payable to a Mr E. Daly and is dated April 1808. It could be exchanged for the equivalent in Bank of Ireland notes.

This Cork banknote, resembling a modern cheque, was payable only after twenty-one days had elapsed. Three guineas was the sum payable to a Mr J. Murphy of the city of Cork.

Minted in 1807 this medallion publicised the aims of the Cork Institution, which promoted agriculture and was once located in the Crawford Art Gallery building. Various images of agrarian animals are featured – horses, a cow and a pig. The Cork Institution later became the Royal Cork Institution.

The Cork Exhibition of 1883 was divided into sections for different types of industry. Prize medallions were awarded to the exhibitors judged to be the best in their section. This medallion is beautifully engraved in the Celtic revival style and features the arms of the city. It was presented to the firm of Baker & Wright for their perfect coffee.

The firm of Carmichael & Co., Patrick Street, issued this advertising token offering twelve months credit in the 1850s. This department store became Cash & Co. in 1877. Brown Thomas continues the tradition of trading on this site today.

A 1929 currency commission £5 ploughman note issued by the Munster & Leinster Bank. The Munster & Leinster bank was located at Nos 63–66 South Mall. In 1929 it had authorised capital of £1,250,000.

This Cork penny, showing a very early example of the arms of the city, was minted in 1659, just thirty-one years before the siege of Cork. Over the years various examples of the coat of arms were designed, but the two castles and the ship remained, proclaiming Cork as a safe harbour for ships.

Unofficial farthings, such as this one, were in use in Cork from the early 1800s. E. Cleburne used this advertising token to promote his woollen drapery business located at No. 9 Great George Street (now Washington Street).

An extremely rare high value £10 note issued by the Munster & Leinster Bank. The bank was established in 1885 and it had the unenviable reputation of having to be rescued from insolvency by Murphy's Brewery proprietor James J. Murphy. The Munster & Leinster Bank issued its own banknotes, in conjunction with the other consolidated banks. These notes are known as ploughman notes because of the wonderful scenes depicted. This early example is dated 7 March 1938.

C & J. O'SULLIVAN
MERCHANTS

Blarney Lane,
Cork, Jany 5th 1894

Messrs Sparks & Sons
Arundel

Dear Sirs

We beg to acknowledge receipt
of yours enclosing Cheque
for _____ Five _____ Pounds
11/10 stg for which we feel obliged
Trusting to a continuance of your
favors, which shall always receive our
personal attention

Yours truly,
C & J. O'Sullivan

£6. 11. 10

MILITARY
AND HUNTING
SADDLERS.
R DAY & SON
ESTABLISHED A.D. 1830
AND SADDLERS
IRONMONGERS

DUBLIN 1882
RELIANCE
GOLD MEDAL

TWO PRIZE ME

DEDUCTIONS FROM THIS INVOICE CANNOT BE ENTERTAINED UNLESS ADVISED ON RECEIPT OF GOODS

TRADE
MARK

Sold to

MR W PIGGOTT
WAREHOUSE
GORT
CO GALWAY

TERMS 3¾ CASH 2½ IN 3 MONTHS.

1 DOZ	BAG NEEDLES
1 "	RISEAGLE PIPES
3 ONLY	

PT

E

TELEGRAMS-
"HARRINGTON, CORK."

ESTABL

muman

FITZG-
Shirtmaker, H
44, PATRI

Cheques and Post Office Orders payable

Small accounts are furnished every month, and run
is the limit of credit

CORK

Capt F. L. Duncan
94

DR. TO
Cork Chem
PROPRIETORS OF
KILOH & COMPANY, LTD.
AND
HARRINGTONS BRUSH FACTORY.

13
14
15

7
8
21B/3
1¼

Invoices

PORTMANTEAUS.
…ERLAND TRUNKS
…HAT CASES.
…VELLING BAGS.
…AND SPURS.
…& SADDLES
…E AND

…ERSONALLY SELECTED OR SENT TO ORDER ARE NOT RETURNABLE

…wyers & Co. LTD.
MANUFACTURERS AND
WHOLESALE WAREHOUSEMEN

…RK, 27TH FEBRUARY 1930

…SHOW AND STOCK ROOMS:
…MIDDLE ABBEY STREET, DUBLIN.

TELEGRAMS: "DWYER - CORK"

| | 1 | 4 | |

TELEPHONES
164 AND 165.

5.

TELEPHONE: 362

Roches Stores Ltd
CORK

CASH ONLY—AT HALF USUAL RATE OF PROFIT

M _Mrs Sweeney_

Sold by   Exd. by   Date _7/7/…_

4 ft. Wad

CORK GAS CONSUMERS' COMPANY,
OFFICES, 72, SOUTH MALL.

M _Christ Church_   _South Main St_
                                              Dr.

Occupiers are required to give notice of their intention of leaving houses, as they will be held liable for Gas Rental until the Company receives such notice.

No Receipts are valid unless on the Company's Printed Form, and countersigned by the Secretary or Accountant.
Cheques to be made payable to the Company, and crossed.

L.W.C.

INDEX OF METER IN HUNDREDS OF CUBIC FEET

HUNDREDS.   TENS.   UNITS.

The Gas Company recommends every Consumer to keep his own register of the quantity of Gas consumed. If this be done frequently, any waste caused by escapes, or the extravagant use of Gas, will be detected.

If the state of the index is written down at two different periods, and the first reading subtracted from the second, the remainder, with two cyphers added, represents the consumption in the interval. Thus, in the above diagram, the index stands at 7 3 6, add to this two cyphers, and it …me 73,600, or seventy-three thousand six hundred.

			A1 per 1,000 Cubic Feet.	£	s.	d.
	60	Light Meter				
Index		312.500				
Former reading		296.600				
Consumption		15.900	3s. 4d.	2	13	
	50	Light Meter				
Index		71.500				
Former reading		62.2.00				

1899 From   1900 To   _Decr. Mch 31_

& …
…THREE
…CO

These invoices, advertising postcards and signs represent some of Cork's best-known and loved institutions. These examples give us an insight into some of Cork's old businesses through their unique decorative styles.

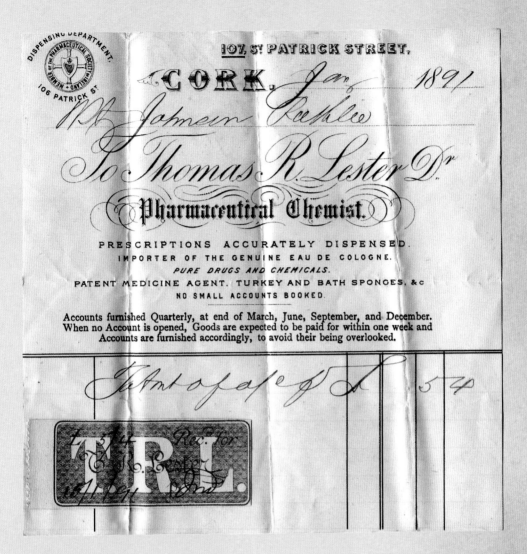

The old Cork pharmaceutical firm of Thomas Lester was located at No. 107 Patrick Street. It was trusted by generations of Cork citizens to dispense prescriptions for all types of ailments. Lester's stocked a bewildering array of medicines, including the once famous Daniel O'Connell ointment, which miraculously cured back ailments.

Opposite: Definitely one of the finest surviving Cork invoices, issued by the firm of Robert Day & Son. Its premises were located at No. 103 Patrick Street – the façade has now been incorporated into the Dunnes Store building. Its factory was located at Bowling Green Street and manufactured all types of equestrian equipment of the highest quality. At the Cork Exhibition of 1883 the firm won two prize medals.

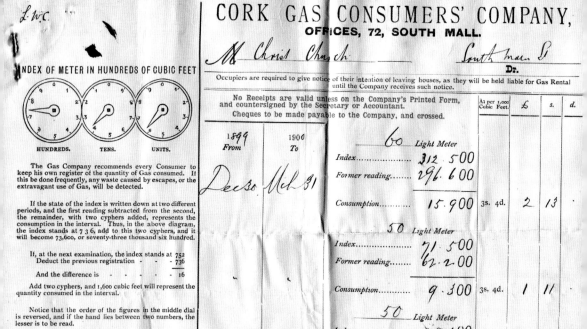

INDEX OF METER IN HUNDREDS OF CUBIC FEET

HUNDREDS.   TENS.   UNITS.

The Gas Company recommends every Consumer to keep his own register of the quantity of Gas consumed. If this be done frequently, any waste caused by escapes, or the extravagant use of Gas, will be detected.

If the state of the index is written down at two different periods, and the first reading subtracted from the second, the remainder, with two cyphers added, represents the consumption in the interval. Thus, in the above diagram, the index stands at 7 3 6, add to this two cyphers, and it will become 73,600, or seventy-three thousand six hundred.

If, at the next examination, the index stands at 752
Deduct the previous registration - - - 736

And the difference is - - - - - 16

Add two cyphers, and 1,600 cubic feet will represent the quantity consumed in the interval.

Notice that the order of the figures in the middle dial is reversed, and if the hand lies between two numbers, the lesser is to be read.

CAUTION.—Never take a light near the Meter. In case of an escape, turn off the Main Cock, open the Windows, and send for your Gasfitter IMMEDIATELY.

If one house has good light, every other house in the neighbourhood should have it equally good, except for some LOCAL defect, which can be quickly remedied IF THE CONSUMER WILL APPLY TO THE GAS COMPANY, who request that any deficiency of light may be immediately notified to them.

CORK GAS CONSUMERS' COMPANY,
OFFICES, 72, SOUTH MALL.

M Christ Church   South Main St.
                                              Dr.

Occupiers are required to give notice of their intention of leaving houses, as they will be held liable for Gas Rental until the Company receives such notice.

No Receipts are valid unless on the Company's Printed Form, and countersigned by the Secretary or Accountant.
Cheques to be made payable to the Company, and crossed.

	1899 From	1900 To		At per 1,000 Cubic Feet.	£	s.	d.
			60 Light Meter				
Index			312.500				
Former reading	Dec 30	Mch 31	296.600				
Consumption			15.900	3s. 4d.		2	13
			50 Light Meter				
Index			71.500				
Former reading			62.200				
Consumption			9.300	3s. 4d.		1	11
			50 Light Meter				
Index			175.700				
Former reading			163.200				
Consumption			12.500	3s. 4d.		2	1	8
					£ 6	5	8

N.B.—When paying this Account, please demand a Printed Receipt from the Collector.

CHEAP FUEL—COKE.

Coke is a superior and economical fuel for all purposes requiring a clean, clear, and strong heat; for drying corn, raising steam, but more especially for household and culinary purposes it is admirably adapted, as it burns without producing any smoke. As kitchen fuel, Coke has long been in use in the principal Hotels in the City, and if more known, would soon be brought into general consumption.

Orders to the Works or to the Office will be promptly attended to.

J. MAHONY, PRINTER, COOK-ST., CORK.

This Cork Gas Consumers' Company invoice dates to March 1900 and it was addressed to Christ Church, South Main Street. It warned not to take a meter reading using a light with a naked flame, for obvious reasons. The company's main office was at No. 72 South Mall.

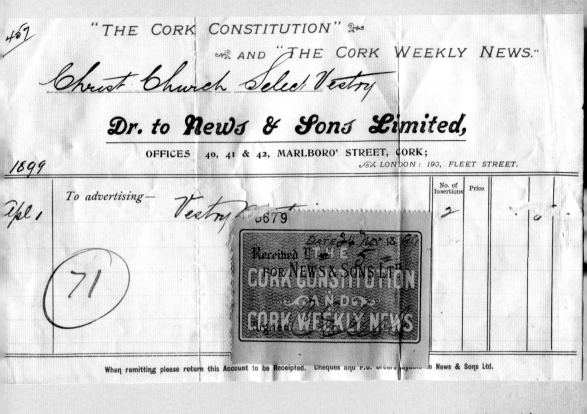

To advertising— *Vestry* 5679

71

	No. of Insertions	Price
	2	

Received for NEWS & SONS Ltd

DATE 24 May 18

THE CORK CONSTITUTION AND CORK WEEKLY NEWS

When remitting please return this Account to be Receipted. Cheques and P.O. orders payable to News & Sons Ltd.

The Cork Constitution was a Protestant newspaper in direct competition with its Catholic counterpart *The Cork Examiner*. This billhead dates to 1899 and is for two insertions by Christ Church select vestry. The paper ceased circulation in 1924, but the name survives today in Cork Constitution Rugby Club.

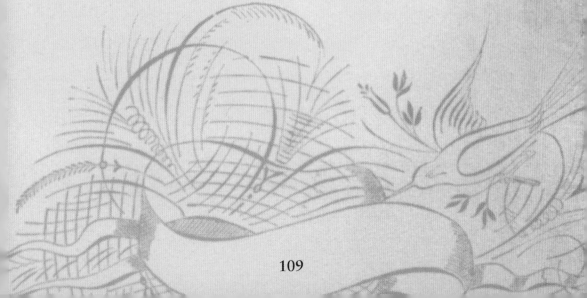

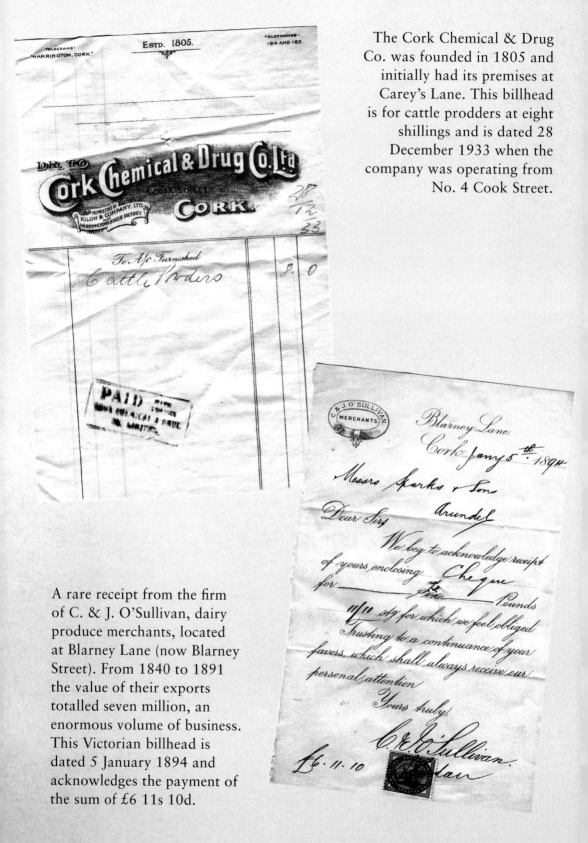

The Cork Chemical & Drug Co. was founded in 1805 and initially had its premises at Carey's Lane. This billhead is for cattle prodders at eight shillings and is dated 28 December 1933 when the company was operating from No. 4 Cook Street.

A rare receipt from the firm of C. & J. O'Sullivan, dairy produce merchants, located at Blarney Lane (now Blarney Street). From 1840 to 1891 the value of their exports totalled seven million, an enormous volume of business. This Victorian billhead is dated 5 January 1894 and acknowledges the payment of the sum of £6 11s 10d.

A lithographed billhead from the firm of Lalor Ltd, which traded at No. 12 Cook Street. They were church candle manufacturers (presumably the reason for the beehive in their lithograph) and oil refiners.

IRISH TRADE MARK NO. 0411.

TELEPHONE Nº 416.

Lalor. Ltd.
CHURCH CANDLE MANUFACTURERS
AND OIL REFINERS
12 COOK STREET. CORK.

With

ts & Thanks

Lalor. Ltd.

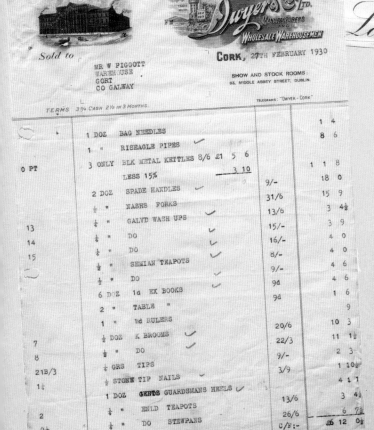

Dwyers & Co LTD.
MANUFACTURERS AND
WHOLESALE WAREHOUSEMEN
CORK, 27TH FEBRUARY 1930

Sold to
MR W PIGGOTT
WAREHOUSE
GORT
CO GALWAY

SHOW AND STOCK ROOMS:
63, MIDDLE ABBEY STREET, DUBLIN.

TELEGRAMS: "DWYER - CORK"

TERMS 3% CASH 2½ IN 3 MONTHS.

				1	4
1 DOZ	BAG NEEDLES			8	6
1 "	RISEAGLE PIPES	✓			
3 ONLY	BLK METAL KETTLES 8/6 £1 5 6			1 1	8
	LESS 15%	3 10		18	0
2 DOZ	SPADE HANDLES	9/-	15	9
½ "	NASHS FORKS	31/6	3	4½
¼ "	GALVD WASH UPS	13/6	3	9
¼ "	DO	15/-	4	0
¼ "	DO	16/-	4	0
¼ "	SEMIAN TEAPOTS	8/-	4	6
¼ "	DO	9/-	4	6
6 DOZ	1d EX BOOKS	9d	1	6
2 "	TABLE "	9d		9
1 "	1d RULERS			
½ DOZ	K BROOMS	20/6	10	3
¼ "	DO	22/3	11	1½
¼ GRS	TIPS	9/-	2	3
¼ "	STONE TIP NAILS	3/9	1	10½
			4	11
1 DOZ	GENTS GUARDSMANS HEELS ✓			
¼ "	ENLD TEAPOTS	13/6	3	4½
¼ "	DO STEWPANS	26/6	6	7½
		C/F:—	£6 12	0½

The firm of Dwyer & Co. literally sold everything from a needle to an anchor. An invoice dated 27 February 1930 lists needles, pipes, kettles and rules. The firm also had an extensive showroom at Middle Abbey Street, Dublin. Their trademark was the beautifully lithographed picture of Blackrock Castle on the top right of the invoice.

27-2-190 1

M Christ Church

Bo.^T OF LONDON & NEWCASTLE
Tea Company.

94. PATRICK STREET. CORK · 56. WILLIAM S.^T LIMERICK.
55. GLADSTONE S.^T CLONMEL · 9. WILLIAM S.^T GALWAY.

& BRANCHES THROUGHOUT ENGLAND. SCOTLAND & IRELAND.

The London & Newcastle Tea Company was located next door to the *Cork Examiner* office on Patrick Street. They also had three other branches at Limerick, Clonmel and Galway. This receipt dates to 1901, a time when tea was a very expensive commodity in Cork.

TELEPHONE: 362

Roches Stores Ltd
CORK

ᴳSH ONLY—AT HALF USUAL RATE OF PROFIT

Sold by   Exd. by   Date

00748 - 13

This Roches Stores receipt lacks the finesse of earlier times, due to a shortage of paper during the years of the Second World War (1939–1945). The astronomical sum of £32 10s was paid for a bed and bedroom furniture, which was delivered to Gardiner's Hill.

The firm of Joseph Mayne was located next door to Robert Day & Son. Mayne's sold glass and china ware and specialised in made to order goods for their select customers. During the 1902–3 Cork exhibition they manufactured cups, plates trinket boxes, etc., as souvenirs of this grand event. This receipt dates to 1902.

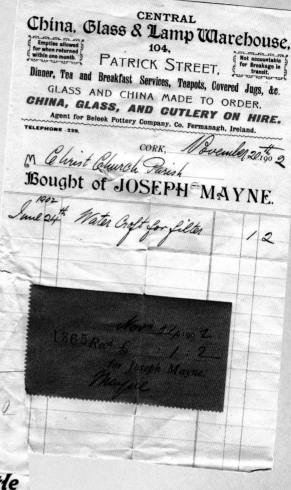

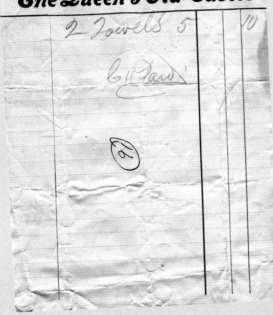

Another old Cork institution is represented by this receipt dating to 1900. T. Lyon & Co. was the precursor of the Queen's Old Castle, which was named in honour of Queen Victoria during her silver jubilee. It was actually located on the site of the King's Old Castle which is represented on the Cork coat of arms. The company sold upholstery, house furnishings, drapery, carpets, silk and jewellery.

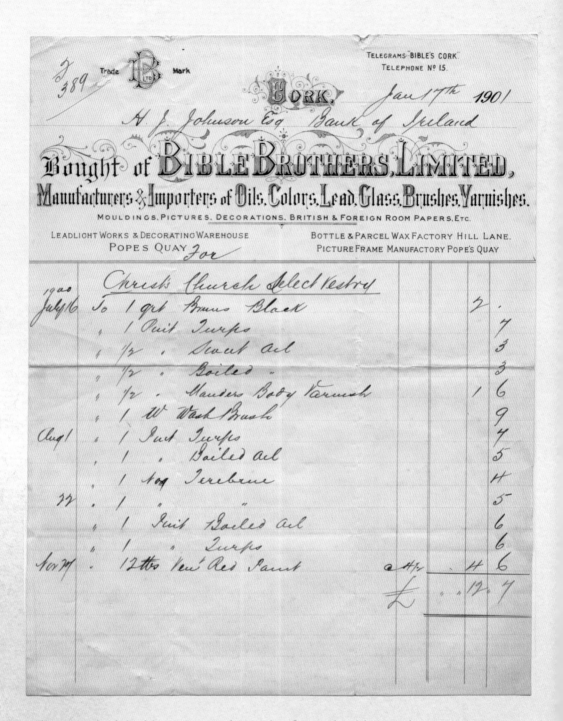

389

TELEGRAMS "BIBLE'S CORK"
TELEPHONE No 15.

CORK, Jan 17th 1901

H. J. Johnson Esq Bank of Ireland

Bought of BIBLE BROTHERS, LIMITED,

Manufacturers & Importers of Oils, Colors, Lead, Glass, Brushes, Varnishes,

MOULDINGS, PICTURES, DECORATIONS, BRITISH & FOREIGN ROOM PAPERS, Etc.

LEADLIGHT WORKS & DECORATING WAREHOUSE
POPES QUAY For

BOTTLE & PARCEL WAX FACTORY HILL LANE.
PICTURE FRAME MANUFACTORY POPE'S QUAY

Christ Church Select Vestry

1900					
July 16	To 1 qrt Bruns Black			2	.
"	1 Pint Turps				7
"	1/2 " Sweet Oil				3
"	1/2 " Boiled "				3
"	1/2 " Flanders Body Varnish			1	6
"	1 W Wash Brush				9
Aug 1	" 1 Pint Turps				7
"	1 " Boiled Oil				5
"	1 tog Terebene				4
"	" 1 " "				5
"	" 1 Pint Boiled Oil				6
"	" 1 " Turps				6
Nov 21	" 12 tbs Ven Red Paint	@ 4½		4	6
		£		12	7

This wonderful old receipt is from the firm of Bible Brothers, Pope's Quay. This well-established old firm manufactured and supplied oils, colours, lead glass, brushes and picture frames. They relocated to the bottom of Shandon Street, where Nosa O'Keeffe's sweet shop, beloved of generations of children and adults alike, later traded.

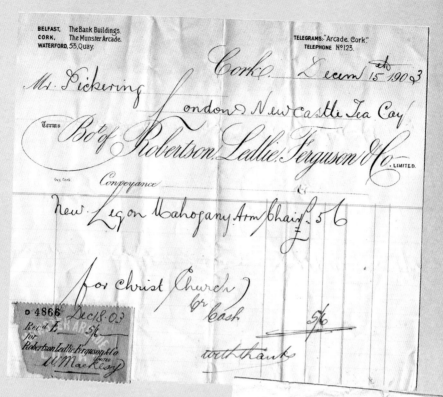

Robertson, Ledlie, Ferguson & Co. traded as the Munster Arcade. This premises was destroyed during the burning of Cork in 1920. Fortunately they rose phoenix-like from the ashes. The initial claim for damages from the British government was for £405,000 but eventually only £213,647 was awarded.

One of the oldest surviving Cork premises is Fitzgerald's Menswear at No. 44 Patrick Street. This company was established as early as 1860, and this invoice is dated to 1894. Credit terms were given monthly, with six months being the maximum term given. Michael Flynn was the then proprietor of this famous gent's outfitter.

Advertising

Cork businesses used every means at their disposal to market and promote their enterprises. Postcards were a popular medium as they could be produced quite cheaply, and if posted in the city in the morning the client would receive it on the same day by evening post. Other types of advertising included calendars, signs, brochures and even commemorative stamps. Here we have a typical comic postcard printed by the Irish Pictorial Card Company. One can only imagine that whatever dollop of magic hair-restorer was applied, it certainly could not produce the golden tresses of the female depicted!

Keep your hair on

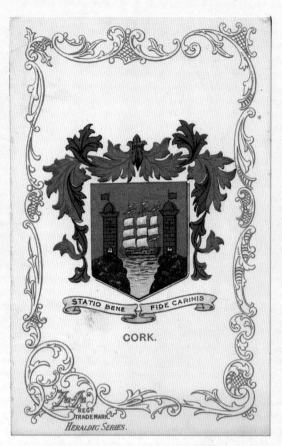

STATIO BENE FIDE CARINIS

CORK.

HERALDIC SERIES.

A wonderful, vibrant postcard depicting the Cork coat of arms. Part of a heraldic series showing the crests of cities of Ireland, the card was printed in Britain *c.* 1915.

Opposite: The Quaker firm of Newsom & Sons Ltd had its main warehouse at French Church Street. Established as early as 1817, tea, coffee, sugar and wholesale food were their main products. This card, advertising instant coffee, one of their most popular products, dates to *c.* 1905.

CLEAN, DURABLE, CHEAP.

TELEPHONE. Nos 3 & 19.

SUTTON'S Compressed Coal.

TELEGRAMS. "SUTTON, CORK"

MANUFACTURED AT OUR FACTORY, LAPP'S QUAY.

All our Coals are selected with the greatest care, and prompt attention paid to each order immediately it is received.

SUTTON'S LTD. Head Office, 1, SOUTH MALL, CORK.

An advertising card from the firm of Sutton's of No. 1 South Mall. Compressed coal, similar to today's briquettes, was manufactured at their factory on Lapp's Quay.

T. O'Gorman & Son Ltd was located in Exchange Street, Cork. They manufactured the Shandon brand of hats, caps, braces and berets. Established in
1904, they exported to England, Germany, Finland, Sweden and America. This
card dates to the early years of their business.

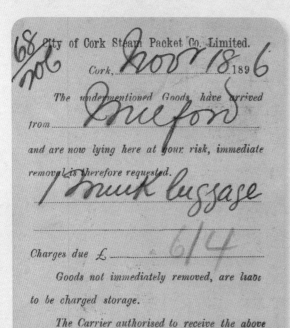

City of Cork Steam Packet Co. Limited.

Cork, _Nov 18_ 189_6_

The undermentioned Goods have arrived

from _Milford_

and are now lying here at your risk, immediate

removal is therefore requested.

1 Trunk luggage

Charges due £ _6/4_

Goods not immediately removed, are liable

to be charged storage.

The Carrier authorised to receive the above

must produce this notice, signed by the Consignee

as an order to the Company for the delivery of

Goods.

_____ { Signature of
                 { Consignee.

This Cork Steam Packet Company notice is dated 18 November 1896 and it requests the owner of a trunk/luggage to retrieve it immediately. The charge due upon collection was six shillings and fourpence. Since it is not signed, we don't know if the luggage was ever collected.

The Savoy advertising card below was issued to promote the film *Top of the Form* starring Ronald Shiner, a well-known British comedian. This film was a 1953 British historical comedy and Shiner played the part of Professor Fortesque. It was obviously a hit, as the *Irish Catholic* newspaper recorded that the audience was in stitches.

DO YOU REALLY WANT TO LAUGH?
DO YOU REALLY WANT TO BE ENTERTAINED?

THEN YOU MUST SEE

RONALD SHINER IN

TOP OF THE FORM

"The audience around me was in stitches" . . . . Irish Catholic.

"If you have any sense of humour this picture will bring it out" Sunday Independent.

"It is quite a while since I heard an audience laugh so wholeheartedly.
                                                    Evening Herald.

SHOWING AT THE SAVOY CINEMA, CORK

Mon., Tues., Wed., 6th, 7th, 8th April

POST CARD

THE ADDRESS ONLY TO BE WRITTEN ON THIS

E Crawley Esq
A Squadron
12th Royal Lancers
Cork Victoria Barracks

A plain postcard from 1896 which was sent to E. Crawley, A Squadron of the 12th Royal Lancers, Victoria Barracks. The card was obviously not collected, as it was redirected to White's Club, St James Street, London. Victoria Barracks, renamed Michael Barracks in 1922 and later Collins Barracks, was once the main hub of the British military in the city.

DWYER & CO. LTD.

COF/NL

DUBLIN: 63, MIDDLE ABBEY STREET,   **CORK,** 29. 7. 19 44.

Mr E. Stanton, Freshford.

- -

     We are sorry we are unable to do the Staples
and Wood Washboards for your esteemed order.
Kindly repeat in future orders.

An order card from Dwyer & Co., issued in the latter years of the Second World War. William Dwyer began a textile business in 1928, which developed into the Sunbeam textile company that closed in 1995. The staples and washboards could not be supplied due to wartime shortages of raw materials. It appears that the company also supplied hardware products.

ALCOCK'S
Delicious
. . Tea

STANDS UNRIVALLED FOR

UNIFORM QUALITY

And *FLAVOUR.*

Wholesale Dept.—

14, BROWN STREET,

CORK.

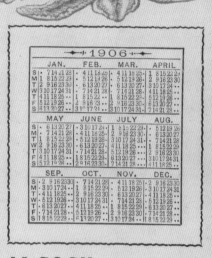

ALCOCK,

Tea Importer,

CORK.

The firm of Alcock's used this miniature calendar to advertise its products in 1906. Alcock's tea was available as a premium blend from the wholesale department of No. 4 Brown Street.

Sutton's hardware department on the South Mall was one of the first businesses to have a phone installed on its premises (telephone

HARDWARE DEPARTMENT.

Telephone No 3.

SUTTONS LIMITED SOUTH MALL, CORK.

Date,....10th June, 1944.

Dear Sirs,

We beg to acknowledge your order for

.....................Hardware................ per ....Post..................

to be deliverded per (XXXXXXXXX (Rail) (XXX (BXXX

Please note orders can only be accepted subject to our being able to supply, and to goods being invoiced at the prices ruling at time of despatch.

Yours faithfully,

SUTTONS LIMITED.

No. 3). Goods were dispatched through the very efficient rail network that existed in Cork and its surrounds, but could also be delivered by lorry, bus or boat for the customer's convenience. Coal, seed, animal feed and general hardware was sold by this company.

An original advertising card from *c.* 1903 for the Shamrock Bakery & Tea Stores, which traded at No. 3 Grand Parade and Ballincollig. Cork had many wonderful bakeries such as Simcox and Thompson's, O'Shea's, and Ormond and Ahern's to name but a few.

A Victorian stamp embossed postcard to the value of one halfpenny – the Victorian version of prepaid envelopes. These order cards were distributed by the City of Cork Steam Packet Company's agents and were then returned, placing orders for coal, etc.

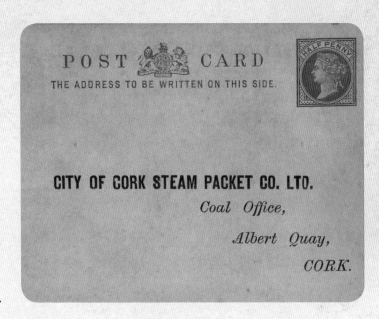

POST ✦ CARD

THE ADDRESS TO BE WRITTEN ON THIS SIDE.

HALF PENNY

CITY OF CORK STEAM PACKET CO. LTD.

Coal Office,

Albert Quay,

CORK.

POST CARD.

Emerald Series, Printed in Ireland.

INLAND ½D.
FOREIGN 1D.

with nothing but address on this side.

FOR INLAND POSTAGE ONLY THIS SPACE MAY BE USED FOR COMMUNICATION.
(Post Office Regulation).

FOR ADDRESS ONLY.

Dear Sirs,

Kindly post me one of your 'SPECIAL ADVERTISING PACKETS containing 72 Penny Pictorial Post Cards. I agree to remit you the Cash for every Card sold, and return you any unsold within four weeks from this date. Children under 14 years must have their parents consent

Name _____

Address _____

TO THE IRISH

PICTORIAL CARD CO,

9, MAYLOR STREET,

CORK.

The Emerald series of postcards were printed by the Irish Pictorial Card Company at No. 9 Maylor Street. This advertising card could be returned requesting seventy-two one-penny postcards for resale. Many of their earlier postcards were badly printed and lacking in detail.

These are three original bottle labels from Beamish & Crawford. The green label advertises An Tóstal stout, which dates it to 1953. The other stout label and the porter label are earlier, and the porter label has the Cork Porter Brewery as the bottler.

Murphy's Brewers, like many other companies, used the arms of Cork as part of their trademark. Murphy's stout was bottled at the brewery, but it was also bottled by agents such as Woodford Bourne's at their premises in Daunt Square. These labels date to the first half of the twentieth century.

St Patrick's Day postcards, such as this one designed in the Celtic revival style, were very popular with Irish emigrants, and were often sent to them by friends and relatives at home.

A very early greeting card printed by the Cork printer Francis Guy, the founding member of the Guy printing empire. The New Year's Day card is printed in both Irish and English and is dated to 1876.

John Rearden & Son was established in 1835 at Great George Street (Washington Street) and sold all types of wine, spirits and beer, as well as being tea dealers. Their representative, Mr J. McCarthy, would have presented this card to customers.

Wm Egan & Sons Ltd

THIRTY-TWO...
PATRICK STREET CORK

2. Ex + part

27 - 10 - '16

Please send us the leaflet for a missal for "All Souls Day." This is a new leaflet got out since the latest regulations.

Kindly send Offices B. V. M ordered some time ago.

obliged
Wm Egan & Sons Ltd

The long-established firm of Egan & Sons Ltd produced some of the finest silver ever created in the city. This card shows they also provided all types of missals. Celtic-design jewellery, such as Tara Brooches, is advertised in their official catalogue below. The firm of William Egan ceased to produce silver in 1986.

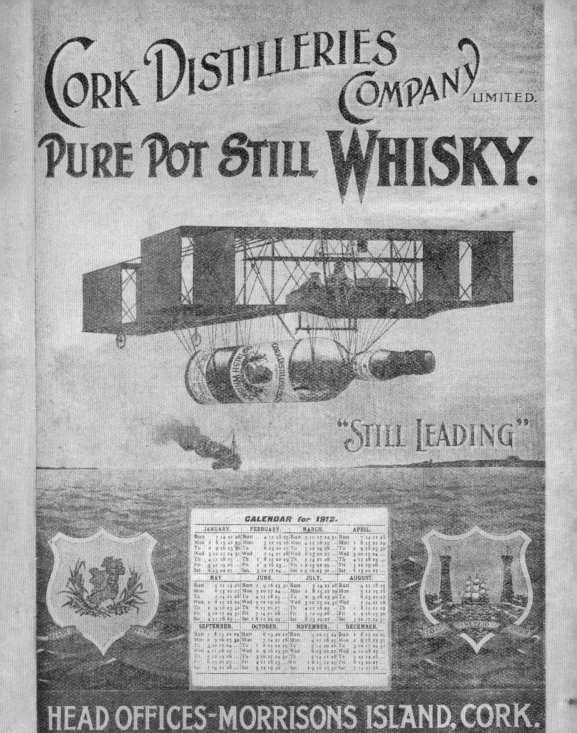

This interesting advertisement comes from a Guy's Directory of 1912. A Cork Distilleries bottle of whiskey being suspended from a primitive aeroplane is a portent of what was to come. Just two years after this appeared the First World War was declared, unleashing the greatest mechanised slaughter the world had ever witnessed. Aeroplanes played their part, dropping bombs from high up in the skies to devastating effect.

New hats can be made up from these models in the
following colours :

Navy, Nigger, Black, Wine, Bottle Green, Grey, Brown

Wool Felts ... ... 30/- Trimmed

Fur Felts ... ... £2 10s. 0d. Trimmed

Models can be tried on in all our Receiving Offices

**HEAD FITTING SIZES
ARE MARKED IN INCHES**

To get the correct measurement of
the head, measurement should be
taken round the crown as indicated
by the measuring tape.

★ PLEASE STATE NUMBER AND
SIZE WHEN ORDERING

This brochure was issued by the firm of R. & J. McKechnie. Old hats could be remodelled to any of the new styles contained within. The famous Cork artist, Gladys Leach, drew the sketches.

Overleaf: This advertising calendar was printed by Guy & Co. for Blackthorn House in 1919. The picture portrays a thronged Patrick Street in all its glory. To the right are the ornate gas lamps of Cash's department store. Just one year later this scene was one of mass destruction when the Black and Tans, the Auxiliaries, RIC and crown soldiers burned the centre of the city.

CALENDAR 1919.

JANUARY.	FEBRUARY.	MARCH.
S M T W T F S	S M T W T F S	S M T W T F S
... ... 1 2 3 4	 1	 1
5 6 7 8 9 10 11	2 3 4 5 6 7 8	2 3 4 5 6 7 8
12 13 14 15 16 17 18	9 10 11 12 13 14 15	9 10 11 12 13 14 15
19 20 21 22 23 24 25	16 17 18 19 20 21 22	16 17 18 19 20 21 22
26 27 28 29 30 31 ...	23 24 25 26 27 28 ...	23 24 25 26 27 28 29
		30 31 ... ...

APRIL.	MAY.	JUNE.
S M T W T F S	S M T W T F S	S M T W T F S
... ... 1 2 3 4 5	... ... 1 2 3	1 2 3 4 5 6 7
6 7 8 9 10 11 12	4 5 6 7 8 9 10	8 9 10 11 12 13 14
13 14 15 16 17 18 19	11 12 13 14 15 16 17	15 16 17 18 19 20 21
20 21 22 23 24 25 26	18 19 20 21 22 23 24	22 23 24 25 26 27 28
27 28 29 30	25 26 27 28 29 30 31	29 30 ... ...

PATRICK STRE...

The original enamel signs for two of Cork's most prominent hardware merchants. The first is for the Cork Iron & Hardware Co. Ltd, located at 15–16 North Main Street and Kyle Street. This wholesale hardware merchants had extensive showrooms; radios, electrical goods, furniture, fireplaces and plumbing materials were also stocked. The second sign is for Eustace & Co. Ltd, established in 1740 and located in Leitrim Street. Joinery, timber, hardware, household goods, wallpaper, oils, clay goods and creosote were all provided by this Cork company.

RYAN'S KELTIC SOAP.

PRIZE MEDAL.

CORK EXHIBITION, 1883.
Telegraphic Address—
"STEARIC, CORK."

EDWARD RYAN & CO., LTD.,
.. *Soap. Candle and* ..
Glycerine Manufacturers.

POPE'S QUAY, CORK.

(Date as on Postmark).

PRIZE MEDAL.

MUNSTER AND CONNAUGHT
EXHIBITION, 1906
Telephone No. 487.

Our Mr. *G. Murphy* will
have the pleasure of waiting upon you in a few days,
when your orders will be esteemed.

E. RYAN & CO., Ltd.

Ryan's Keltic was a soap, candle and glycerine manufacturer located at Pope's Quay. The quality of their products was so good that they won medals at the 1883 Cork Exhibition and the Munster and Connaught Exhibition in 1906, proudly recalled on this business card presented by G. Murphy, who was presumably a salesperson for the company.

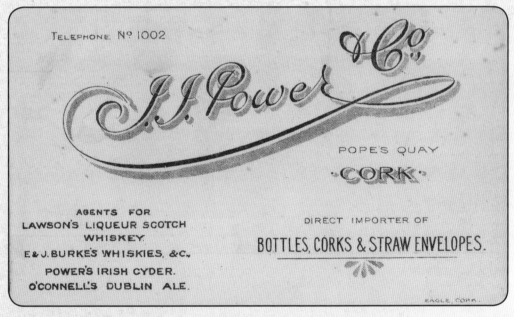

J. J. Power, Pope's Quay, was a wholesale supplier for Scotch whisky, Irish whiskey, ciders and ales. This card was printed by the Eagle Printing Works located in Oliver Plunkett Street.

135

This original press photograph shows the incidents at Marsh's Yard in 1934 where members of the Garda Síochána attacked protesting farmers. One farmer was shot and several were injured when the police baton-charged the crowd.

Military and Police

Throughout its history Cork has had military fortifications established within the city. Elizabeth Fort and Cat Fort were early defensive structures, but were proved largely ineffective during the siege of Cork in 1690 when faced with heavy artillery. By 1801 the threat of a Napoleonic invasion necessitated the building of a new barracks for the city, which was initially named Cork Barracks. It later was renamed Victoria Barracks in honour of Queen Victoria, and following the handing over of the barracks by the British to the Provisional Government in 1922 the name was changed to Michael Barracks and then Collins Barracks in 1925, in honour of Michael Collins. The RIC also had barracks in the city, including stations at the Bridewell, Union Quay and King Street (now MacCurtain Street).

A very rare Cork military letter dated 15 August 1811. The letter was addressed to the mayor of Cork and was written by Captain William Le Grand. It informed the mayor of a proposed march through the city by soldiers of his regiment. The purpose of this exercise was to make them better acquainted with the defences of the city.

This original press photograph shows a ragbag of military personnel and RIC men posing warily for the photographer during the War of Independence. Sandbags, barbed wire and a menacing Lewis gun protrude from the entrance to the Cork Court House. Posters in the background were for Cork County elections, due to take place on 2 June 1920.

IRISH VOLUNTEER BAND, CORK.

The Cork Irish Volunteer Force pipe band dressed in all their nationalist finery. The men shown, left to right, are: (*back row*) M. Trahey, Donal Barrett, Martin Donovan, D. O'Gorman, Tadhg Hegarty; (*centre row*) Seán O'Sullivan, N. Waters, M. McCarthy, D. Hurley, J. Courtney, James Hastings; (*front row*) Daniel Foley, Michael Wickham, Tadhg Barry, William Horan, Louis Courtney, D. McCarthy, Patrick Horan.

A glass lantern photograph showing a more sinister side of life, with a group of policemen posing proudly outside a Cork railway station in the 1890s, labelled 'RIC men returning from an eviction scene'. Note the advertising signs for Alcock's tea and the Crosshaven Hotel in the background.

A lithographed invoice addressed to Tadhg Barry and Thomas MacCurtain at the Irish Volunteer Hall in Sheares Street. The invoice was for various types of printed material, including propaganda and recruiting leaflets. The grand total came to eleven pounds and nine shillings and it is dated Good Friday 1916.

A very imposing view of the square of Victoria Barracks. This regiment is lined up and ready for inspection. During the Civil War most of the barracks was destroyed by anti-Treaty Republicans who set fire to it before they evacuated.

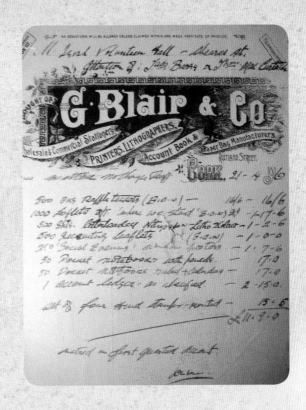

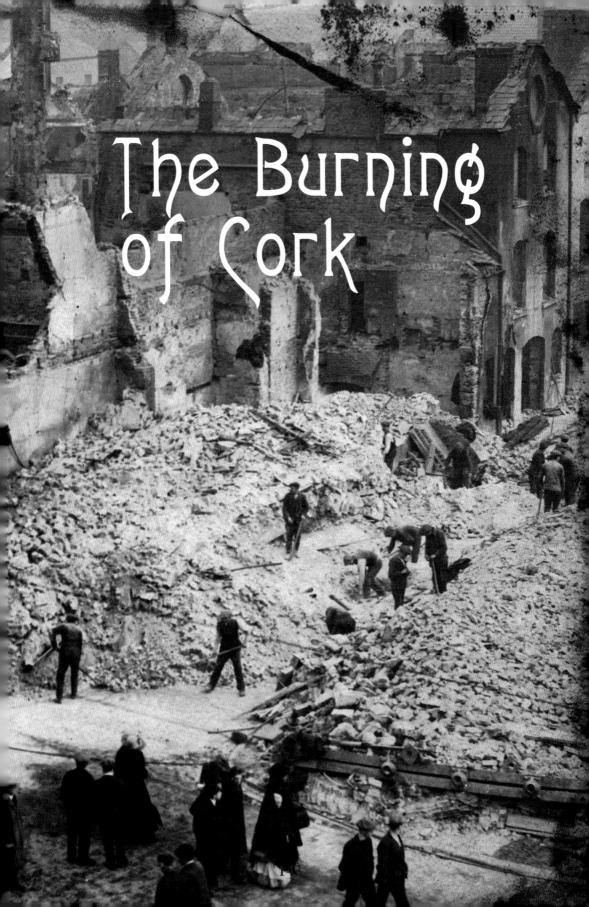

The Burning of Cork

Many books and articles have been written throughout the years concerning the burning of Cork city. This deliberate act of arson and looting by the British military in reprisal for IRA attacks destroyed the commercial heart of the city. Photographs conjure up the devastation far better than words.

Previous page: This photograph shows that the devastation was not confined to the main street of the city. Side streets, such as Maylor Street, shown here, were also badly affected.

The morning after the burning of the commercial heart of the city centre. Cork citizens stare in disbelief at the devastation wreaked on their beautiful city by the RIC, Auxiliaries, Black and Tans and British military on 11 December 1920 in reprisal for IRA attacks on their members.

As Cork citizens wandered about the rubble, it was obvious that little could be salvaged. The twisted wrought-iron supports in the foreground give some idea of the heat which was generated during the inferno.

A fire hose is directed at the smouldering rubble. Such was the build-up of heat that steam and smoke was still being emitted hours after the catastrophic event.

Fortunately the other side of Patrick Street, seen in the top right corner of this image, miraculously escaped the ravages of the burning. The well-established Cork firm of Robert Day & Co. can be seen; the façade is now incorporated into the premises of Dunnes Stores.

Remains of Electric Tram Car after Cork Fire, Dec. 1920

Even travelling on the Cork tramway system was not a safe place to be – passengers, including a local priest, were beaten and had their lives threatened. The tram in this picture was destroyed outside the premises of No. 3 Patrick Street. A contemporary eyewitness account was published by the Irish Labour Party in January 1921 entitled *Who Burnt Cork?*

The passengers travelling on this undamaged Cork tram after the fire had an unobstructed view of the charred remains of the old City Hall. The old bell tower and clock, which were in the centre of the building, collapsed downwards during the inferno and no remains of them appear in view.

Several attempts had been made to set fire to the City Hall before the burning of the city centre. Temporary shutters had been put in place to prevent hand grenades and other incendiary devices being fired through the windows, but these proved ineffective against its determined attackers on this occasion.

After the fire, several temporary premises were erected so that some form of limited trading could take place. The principal commercial premises of Cash & Co., Munster Arcade and William Egan & Sons were to the fore in this venture.

WM. EGAN & SONS, FOREIGN MONEY EXCHANGED.

Miniatures, Enamels, Old Paste Ornaments, Curiosities, Coins. ♦♦♦♦♦

GRANDFATHER CLOCKS.

Watchmakers, Jewellers, and Diamond Merchants.
♦♦♦

Old Cork and Waterford Cut Glass.   Antique China.

ECCLESIASTICAL VESTMENTS AND CHURCH PLATE MANUFACTURERS,

SPECIALITY **ANTIQUE SILVER CURIOS.**

Snuff Boxes, Salts, Cream Ewers, Sugar Bowls, Tea and Coffee Sets, Large Presentation Pieces.   **OLD ENGLISH SILVER.**

ARTISTIC PIECES OF CONTINENTAL MANUFACTURE.

ENGRAVINGS: Coloured, Mezzotint, and Old Line Engravings by the most famous Engravers of the 18th Century. *Collections of different Masters and Galleries.*

We give the Highest Prices for all kinds of Antiques.

32, PATRICK STREET, CORK.

An interesting advertisement from 1903 showing the premises of William Egan, the famous Cork silversmiths. It was several years before the British government paid compensation for the destruction of the business. Fortunately the premises were rebuilt on a grand scale.

MEMORANDUM.

The National Bank Limited,

CORK BRANCH

To All Cashiers

13 DEC 1920   19

Re. the recent outrages against property &c. carried out by local auxiliary forces. Should there be a repetition of lawlesness by the above mentioned the following precautions are to be observed: I. Porters to lock all doors and escort remaining customers to rear of premises. 2. Cashier tills to be secured and counter staff to follow to the rear and remain thus until deemed safe by senior staff to reopen for business. Your cooperation in this matter is essential.

J. R. Hall   MANAGER.

This memo was issued to the staff of the national bank on the South Mall just two days after the burning of the city. Certain precautions were to be taken to ensure the safety of staff and customers alike in the event of another attack. It is obvious from memos like this one that further atrocities were expected to befall Cork city.

The ambush of British forces near Dillon's Cross by the IRA was the catalyst for the crown forces to go on the rampage. The burning, looting and pillaging of city-centre premises and terrorising of citizens and business people was their wanton act of revenge. This picture shows the charred remains of Brian Dillon's house.

On the left of this picture a banner advertising a salvage sale can be seen. The shrewd businessman William Roche had taken precautions against trouble, protecting the stock in his nearby warehouse by covering it with iron sheets. The following day he was transacting business from temporary premises.

The Carnegie Library, adjoining the City Hall, was also targeted and it was destroyed by fire. All of its general stock, including rare printed Cork books and newspapers, were consumed in the conflagration.

People

Bryan Cody, in his book *The River Lee, Cork and the Corkonians* published in 1859, had this flattering opinion of Cork people: 'Passing through the leading thoroughfares of the city during the business hours of the day, the stranger will be struck with the many good-humoured faces he shall meet on his walk. Among all classes he will see countenances rosy with health and beaming with intelligence.' Some of the earlier images here were taken just a few decades after this publication and all of them show the human face of the city.

The Mardyke was a very popular spot for Cork citizens. This early stereo view dates to 1877. Note the dog clasped in the arms of the gentleman on the right, presumably because if the animal was to run about it would have ruined the photograph.

Previous page: Two-way traffic was the order of the day when this photograph was taken in 1927. The donkey and cart and its occupants are located outside Thompson's Bakery on MacCurtain Street. To the right is the Grosvenor Hotel on the corner of York Hill.

This stereo view dates to *c*. 1880 and was taken on the steps of Blair's Hill.
To the left of this image was the entrance to historian and antiquarian John
Windele's home, Blair's Castle. Parts of this image are doubly exposed due to
movement and the long exposure time needed.

Many people posed for this stereo view, dating to *c.* 1890. It was taken outside the North Chapel. At that time the donkey was widely used as a means of transporting goods within the city. The photographer appears to have chosen his moment carefully to capture this magical image.

Some of the differences in social status can be seen in this image: the well-made clothing and fancy top hat of the carriage driver contrasts sharply with the attire of the shoeless urchin leaning against his donkey cart. In the background historic buildings blend beautifully: Finns Corner, Woodford Bourne's and the Queen's Old Castle jostle for primacy.

Bridge Street with Bariscales Jewellers' clock on the left. Bridge Street was the gateway to Patrick Street, and this image dates from 1897, just before the introduction of the electric trams.

A laneway scene off Shandon Street where neighbours gather as a community and their gossip flows as fast as the water from the communal pump. Most seem unaware of the presence of the photographer who has captured this image for posterity.

A busy pedestrian scene at Patrick's Bridge. Note the confidant swagger of the uniformed man in contrast with his fellow citizens. The cobbled stones on the road give no hint of the impending arrival of the electric tram in 1898.

A street scene outside the North Chapel, probably taken on the Sabbath day as everyone seems to be dressed in their finery. Note the immaculate whites and postures of people proud of their faith.

An unusual stereo view taken at Sunday's Well, near the junction to Shanakiel. This appears to be a cart bringing butter to the butter market near Shandon. It dates to 1891 and the topography of the area has changed little since then.

The Mardyke Walk was created in 1719 by Edward Webber and was named after the Meer Dyke in Amsterdam (meaning sea dyke). A bye-law of 1868 relating to the Mardyke stated: 'No person shall ride any horse, pony, mule or donkey on the said Mardyke or drive any sheep, pigs or cattle thereon.'

This Guy & Co. photograph of 1897 shows typical Cork street vendors. These hardy women would have travelled from all over the county and sold their wares, typically at Paddy's Market on Cornmarket Street. These travelling dealers sold a fine array of fish and other produce.

This glass lantern slide was taken outside the premises of John Atkins at No. 54 South Mall. The gentleman in the centre has been identified as a Mr Harrington. Curtis's smokeless cartridges are advertised on the window. Agricultural implements, and what are possibly dried tobacco leaves, were sold at these premises.

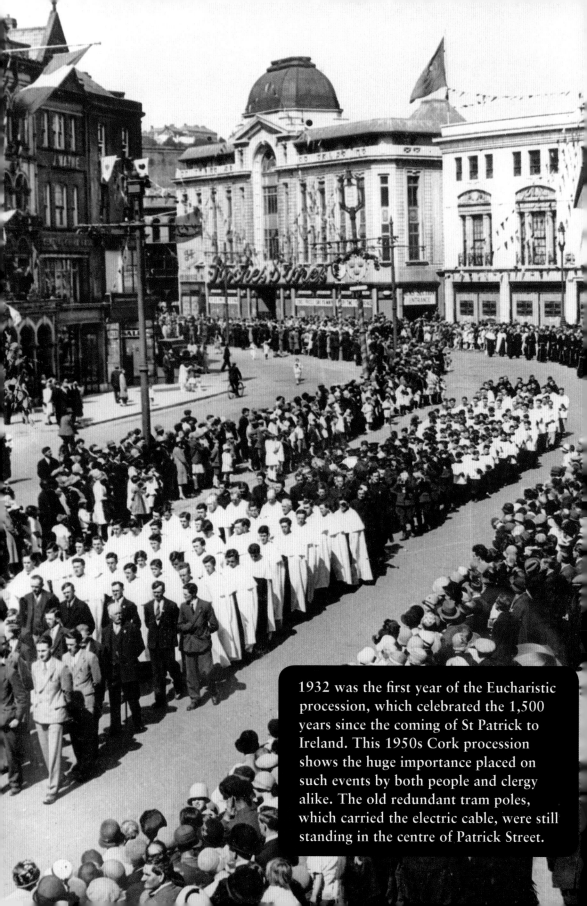

1932 was the first year of the Eucharistic procession, which celebrated the 1,500 years since the coming of St Patrick to Ireland. This 1950s Cork procession shows the huge importance placed on such events by both people and clergy alike. The old redundant tram poles, which carried the electric cable, were still standing in the centre of Patrick Street.

It is hard to imagine that General Eoin O'Duffy could command such a large following. This original press photograph is dated to 1933 and was taken on the Grand Parade. This was the time of a huge political sea change – the Blue Shirts and their fascist salutes were seen by some as a new alternative to traditional democratic values.

John F. Kennedy's arrival in Ireland caused a major sensation – the most powerful man on earth was coming home to his roots. He visited Cork city on his whistle-stop tour. This photograph captures some of this magical moment as crowds thronged Cork's streets waving American flags with great fervour.

out to play

This private picture postcard of the early 1900s shows a boy and girl with two hoops. This image was taken within the grounds of Victoria Barracks. Simple toys were the order of the day: hoops, spinning tops, cork guns and old bicycles were in common use.

This photograph is of my wife's grandfather, Charles Lewis Clark. He enlisted in the British army in Cork on 12 June 1915 at the age of 21, one of over 73,000 Irishmen who enlisted between 1915 and 1918. He fought in France during the First World War in the Leinster Regiment. Unfortunately he was gassed in the trenches and declared medically unfit for further service. He died in 1928 from his medical condition at the age of 34.

Shawlies

An old tradition in Cork was the wearing of a shawl by women, so much so that these women came to be known as Shawlies. Many of the earlier shawls were multi-coloured and patterned as can be seen in the following images. These shawls were of a very practical nature as they could be used for carrying fruit, vegetables, etc. Even young infants could be carried in them and protected from the elements. On November 2010, at the ripe old age of ninety, Mary Ellen Lowther, the city's last Shawlie, passed away and with her died an old Cork custom.

Definitely one of my favourites: the haunting face of a Shawlie, her companion but a blur in the background. Frozen in time – the spar of a sailing ship, the beautiful limestone arches of Patrick's Bridge, Cork's beautiful buildings – it does not get better than this.

Previous page: These Shawlies conveyed their goods to the market in large wicker baskets. The Shawlies had imploring faces, hoping to entice someone to buy. This stereo view dates to *c.* 1880 when Cornmarket Street had a beautiful cobbled walkway.

A view of Paddy's Market published by the American stereo view company, Keystone, in 1896. The Coal Quay has a long tradition associated with the Shawlies. It is interesting to note the different patterns on the shawls worn by the women in the photograph.

This 1903 scene shows a thronged market with every type of produce available. Haggling and bargain hunting were the order of the day, as everything had to be sold – the only alternative was to cart it home. To the left, a huge array of wicker baskets and cots can be seen for sale.

This glass lantern slide dated to 1905 is an excellent example of the photographer's art. People are posing for the camera; baskets of eggs are proudly displayed by the matriarchal figures as the curious onlookers peer into the lens of the camera.

The wicker baskets seen here are fine examples of the type produced by local artisans. The dealers on this occasion are selling garments at a clothes market. No. 39, on the extreme left, was the Beamish & Crawford pub run by Anne O'Donnell, whilst her neighbours on either side were basket makers. By 1908 Cornmarket Street had no less than eleven public houses. This stereo view dates to 1903.

This glass lantern slide, *c.* 1900, shows Coal Quay dealers in their traditional attire of shawls and skirts. These formidable ladies were intent on selling, making it difficult not to buy. The Shawlie on the left appears in fine fettle and looks as if she is about to start dancing.

A gooseberry seller and her little stall in 1911, at the top of Grand Parade. This poor unfortunate looks quite weather-beaten – time and hard work have taken their toll. It was common for these traders to set up stalls on streets or near quay walls to sell fruit to passers-by.

Previous page: An original photograph taken at Cattle Market Street, which belies its date of 1954. Two Shawlies make their way uphill; the shoes of the woman on the left are in tatters, reflecting the poverty that existed in the 1950s. To the right note the old weighing scales and makeshift stall – vegetables were sold from this house to earn a little money.

This traditional clothes market, located on Kyle Street, is the subject of a private photograph taken in July 1938. The curious stares of the Shawlies and customers display uneasiness at having their images captured for posterity.

Opposite: In this photograph the Shawlies have a determined look etched on their faces. The barrels in the foreground suggest that they were selling meat or fish which had been preserved. A sign overhead advertises breakfasts, dinners and snacks. Nine refreshment rooms are recorded as existing in the busy thoroughfare of Cornmarket Street in 1908.

Photographers

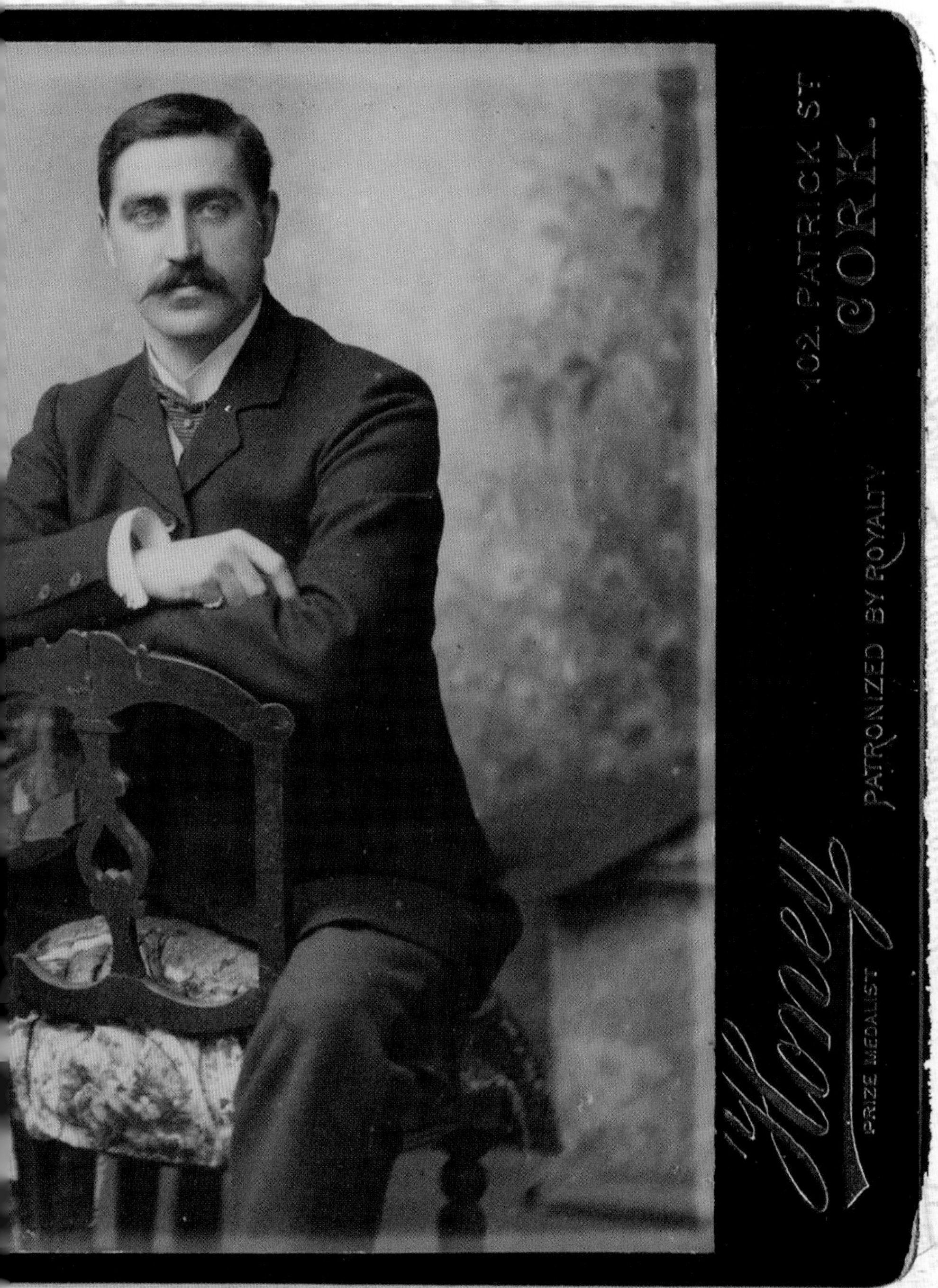

102, PATRICK ST

CORK.

PATRONIZED BY ROYALTY

Honey

PRIZE MEDALIST

Paris Studio 64ᴬ PATRICK ST · CORK ·

Previous page: An early twentieth-century family photograph taken by Honey of No. 102 Patrick Street. There was a long tradition of photographers operating from these premises. By 1904 there were eleven photographic studios in the city centre.

Studio portraits, such as this from the accomplished lens of the Paris Studio, were taken for special occasions.

Hunter · 28. PATRICK ST CORK.

The firm of Hunter photographers operated from the 1860s for many years in their premises at No. 28 Patrick Street. Commercial photographic equipment had become more technologically advanced making it cheaper for people to have their photograph taken.

Mack

28 GRAND PARADE
· CORK ·

This photograph was taken by Mack at No. 28 Grand Parade, *c.* 1900.
Invariably the sitters are dressed in their Sunday best, making them a rich
source for Cork's social history.

CALLAGHAN CORK

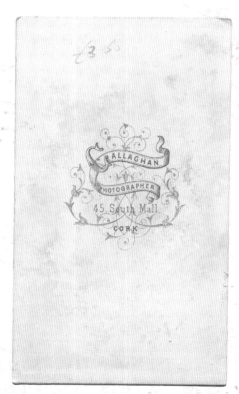

CALLAGHAN
PHOTOGRAPHER
45. South Mall.
CORK

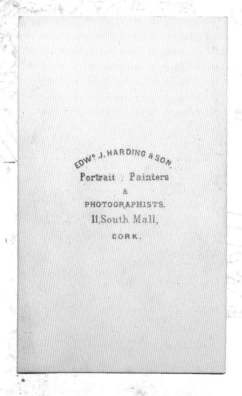

EDW J. HARDING & SON.
Portrait Painters
&
PHOTOGRAPHISTS,
11, South Mall,
CORK.

HARDING & SON CORK.

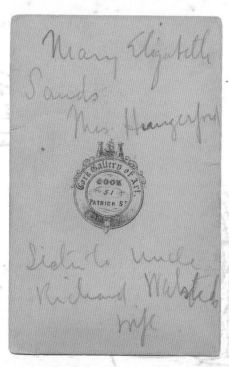

By the early 1860s new advances in technology meant that the *carte de visite,* measuring 2¼ x 4 inches, became the most popular medium of photography. They became known as *cartes de visite,* because these were about the size of a Victorian visiting card.

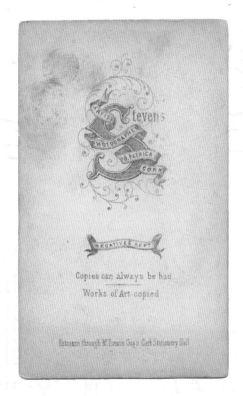

The rear of these cards advertised the studios of the photographer and they could be purchased for approximately twelve shillings and sixpence per dozen, making them affordable for rich and poor alike.

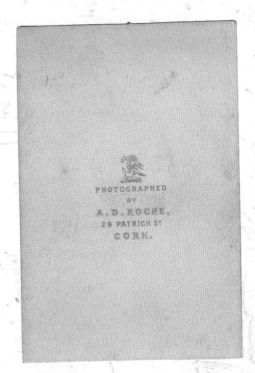

PHOTOGRAPHED
BY
A. D. ROCHE,
29 PATRICK ST
CORK.

R. WARD & Cº   CORK

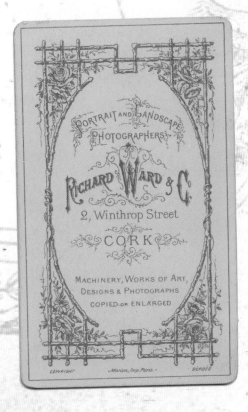

PORTRAIT AND LANDSCAPE
PHOTOGRAPHERS

Richard Ward & Cº

2, Winthrop Street
CORK

MACHINERY, WORKS OF ART,
DESIGNS & PHOTOGRAPHS
COPIED OR ENLARGED

The River Lee

The River Lee was for centuries the main artery into the city and was particularly important for the development of trade in Cork city. The changing face of the city can be seen in the series of images here as the old sailing ships give way to more modern steamships, but many of the bridges and façades of the buildings have survived and provide a direct link with the Cork of more than a century ago. This magnificent panoramic photograph from the 1880s shows the professional skill of the photographer as he has captured the churches of St Finbarre's and St Mary's, Pope's Quay, in the background. The quays are busy, with tall-masted ships loading and discharging their cargos. The old bonded warehouses, in the centre of the photograph, retain their old-world charm.

An early stereo view from 1877 of the Mercy Hospital, formerly the mayor's residence, and the Maltings' building. To the extreme left, the ornate portico was the entrance to Dr Barter's Turkish baths establishment at Grenville Place.

Patrick's Bridge and the old Georgian houses on Camden Quay in 1890. To the right of the bridge Wheeler's pianoforte and music warehouse can be seen. Musical instruments, especially pianos, were very popular and were one of the few forms of entertainment before the advent of radio.

Looking downriver at the masts of the old tall sailing ships evokes memories of a bygone time. Fortunately the old Georgian red brick buildings still stand on Camden Quay. The substantial limestone blocks of the quay walls give some inkling of the laborious task of their construction.

A beautiful early albumen print showing the old higgledy-piggledy buildings that were once part of Merchant's Quay. The tobacco warehouse, the Bridge Saloon, the steamship company's office and MacSwiney's all appear a little neglected.

This hand-coloured glass lantern slide, c. 1890, shows a busy Patrick's Bridge. Note that Mangan's clock is attached to their building. From this image, we can clearly see that the clock started life as a bracket clock before becoming Mangan's pillar clock, which exists to this day.

A clear view of the wide expanse of the River Lee between the North Mall and Bachelor's Quay taken in 1887. The old Georgian buildings to the left are a remnant of the times when the rich merchants of the city resided here.

This 1870 view of early sailing ships berthed on both quays gives a good depiction of Cork as a maritime city. Ships discharged their cargoes right onto the city quays, whilst the nearby railway could convey these goods to all parts of Ireland.

This atmospheric photograph shows two old Cork landmarks, St Finbarre's Cathedral and the old Southgate Bridge. To the right of the cathedral is one of Beamish & Crawford's chimney stacks. This brewery, sadly gone, founded in 1792, was once the largest in Ireland.

This is a very rare image of the old wooden St Vincent Bridge, which existed before the current metal pedestrian bridge and was constructed in 1862. This structure was paid for initially by private subscription thanks to the generosity of Sunday's Well residents. One of the main subscribers was Mr Wyse of Wyse's Distillery, which was one of the prominent employers in the area at this time. The present steel bridge was constructed in 1875.

The age of steam had truly arrived when this photograph was taken in the late 1800s. Note the beautiful bow-fronted building on the left. Its neighbour was the Vulcan Foundry & Engineering Works. The royal arms on the Custom House have since been replaced by the Cork coat of arms.

Much has changed since this photograph of French's Quay and Bishop Street was taken in 1954. The old buildings and Proby's Bridge and Quay look like they are from a far-off time, whilst Elizabeth Fort and St Finbarre's tower over them. The advertising sign on the centre shop is for Clarke's plug and St Bruno's flake tobacco.

This 1950s photograph shows seagulls taking flight from an old mooring on Union Quay. The old buildings on the left contrast sharply with the newer School of Commerce building. The old quay walls have been shored up with long timber beams on both sides.

Ships

Cork harbour was the maritime gateway to the city. This natural harbour was the ideal anchorage for large ships, and the list of ships that anchored here reads like a who's who of shipping. The *Titanic* called to Queenstown (now Cobh) on its ill-fated voyage, while the *Lusitania* was another visitor before being sunk by a German U-Boat near the Old Head of Kinsale on her return to Ireland. Albumen prints, postcards and stereo views give a wonderful insight into some of the magnificent ships that visited Cork. In this image the photographer managed to catch the reflection in the water and the flight of the seagulls. To the left, old sailing ships lie berthed near the new hybrids, the steamships. The wide expanse of the river is clearly living up to its description *statio bene fide carnis* – a safe harbour for ships.

A stereo view *c.* 1880 showing a busy quayside scene with sailing ships discharging a cargo of timber and the old City Hall in the background. Cork had many timber merchants such as Deaves Brothers, Penrose Quay, Eustace's, Leitrim Street, Haughtons, North Main Street, and O'Connell's, Union Quay and South Terrace.

An extremely early Cork stereo view by John England, dated 1859, showing a posed scene. The couple would have had to remain motionless for several minutes for the scene to be captured for posterity. The wooden sailing ship dominates the scene as the merchants' houses of Montenotte look down on the port of Cork.

Another stereo view, from 1887, showing slightly ghostly images of steam and sailing ships at Cork quays. To the extreme left is the Custom House which was designed by Abraham Hargrave in 1814.

The Derwent

CORK, 11 Month, 20 1798
BOUGHT OF *THOMAS HARRIS,*
At his OIL, PAINT, VARNISH, GLASS & LEAD STORES,
Nº. 26, PAUL-STREET.

30 ℔ Ground White Lead @ 6d ℔ 16.7
6 ℔ Black paint 1/6 ..... 9.—
6 ℔ Co Yellow @ 8d 4.0
8 Sea Green @ 2½ 13.0
4 Gs. B Oil 28/ 4 Bladr 4 ..... 1.8.4
1 Keg 4/ 3 Crocks 4/2 ..... 1.4½
..... 3.12.3½
Disct 3.7½
Recd the Contents 3.8.8
Jno Newton

Stereo view, *c.* 1870, showing tall ships in the background and a lifting crane at a Cork quay in the foreground. This scene brings to mind the visit of the tall ships to Cork in 1991.

Opposite: A receipt made payable to the ship *Derwent,* dated 20 November 1798, from the premises of Thomas Harris, No. 26 Paul Street. Among the goods listed are six gallons of black paint at one shilling sixpence, yellow paint at eightpence and pea green paint at two shillings and twopence.

The old paddle steamship *Bristol* berthed outside the offices of the Cork Steam Ship Company at Penrose Quay, *c*. 1880. Ebenezer Pike formed this company in 1843 and it later became the offices of the Cork Steam Packet Company.

eland.—Scot's Church, Cork.

An old sea dog poses near this old steamship. The ghostly apparition of the Scot's church or the Church of the Holy Trinity at Summerhill appears in the background. Early photographs such as this often fade as the natural chemicals erode.

A very busy inner harbour scene from a stereo view, *c.* 1880. Sailing ships still outnumbered steamships quite significantly when this image was taken. A crude type of crane was used to load and discharge cargoes from these ships.

The White Star liner *Celtic* was built by the Belfast firm of Harland and Wolff in 1901. This 20,000-ton liner was one of the largest liners afloat at that time. The *Celtic* was carrying assembly parts for Henry Ford's, refrigerated goods and passengers when she ran aground at Roches Point on 10 December 1928. This black and white slide shows the *Celtic* on the rocks at high tide.

This coloured glass lantern of a quayside scene at Cork was made by an amateur artist in the late nineteenth century. Although the ships docked on the quay look somewhat realistic, Patrick's Bridge and Trinity Church are totally lacking in detail.

THE QUAY, CORK

Another coloured glass lantern slide of Cork harbour, dating to the 1880s, shows the causeway which was created by convict labour to connect Haulbowline with Spike Island. The ship is the wooden-hulled HMS *Revenge*, which was renamed the *Empress* and served as a training ship on the Clyde in 1890.

The *Cormorant* was built for the Cork Steam Ship Company by Wigham Richardson & Co. Ltd of Newcastle in 1900. This steamship was sunk when it struck a mine on October 1914, but fortunately all of her crew survived.

A twin-funnelled paddle steamer berthed at Merchant's Quay in the 1880s. The barrels contain butter, provisions and stout or ale from the local breweries. Paddle steamers could transport huge cargoes by sea, making them a very efficient means of transport.

In 1821 businessmen intent on developing trade between Cork, Dublin and Liverpool founded the St George Steam Packet Company. This nice clear albumen print of Penrose Quay shows the Steam Ship Company building, with a statue of St George slaying the dragon above the pediment. The steamship pictured was twin powered as it could also use sails to increase speed and efficiency.

This is an original quayside scene which was taken privately in 1936. Two men look on as a crane unloads material from the ship. The Cork quays were extremely busy and hundreds of dockers, both full time and casual, were employed to discharge and load cargo. In the 1970s the banana boat and the chocolate crumb boat were very welcome visitors to Cork.

An early albumen print, *c*. 1880, showing
sailing ships at Patrick's Quay. Two paddle
steamers are berthed at Merchant's Quay.
Passenger comfort appears to have been
sparse as the benches in the centre of the
steamers were completely exposed to the
elements.

NEW QUADRUPLE TURBINE   R.M.S. "LUSITANIA"   32,500 TONS, 68,000 HORSE POWER. LENGTH, 785 FT. BREADTH, 88 FT. DEPTH, 60 FT. 6

The 32,000-ton cruise liner *Lusitania* was torpedoed by the German submarine U-20 near the Old Head of Kinsale. Many theories exist as to why she was sunk, and the sinking of this majestic liner certainly accelerated America's entrance into the war on the Allied side. The *Lusitania*, in common with other liners during the First World War, was refitted to accommodate gun turrets. The 'Lusitania Medallion' was privately issued in Germany to mark the sinking of the ship. British copies such as the example below were widely distributed as part of an anti-German campaign.

An advertising postcard for the White Star's liners, the *Olympic* and *Titanic*, which were triple screw 45,000-ton ships, the largest steamers in the world.

An official receipt from Aherne's Exchange and Shipping Office, Queenstown, dated 9 April 1912 for the sum of $225 in the form of a bank draft transferred via the *Titanic*.

WHITE STAR LINE

THE LARGEST STEAMERS IN THE WORLD.

THE LARGEST STEAMERS IN THE WORLD.

"OLYMPIC" (TRIPLE-SCREW), 45,000 TONS,
"TITANIC" (TRIPLE-SCREW), 45,000 TONS.

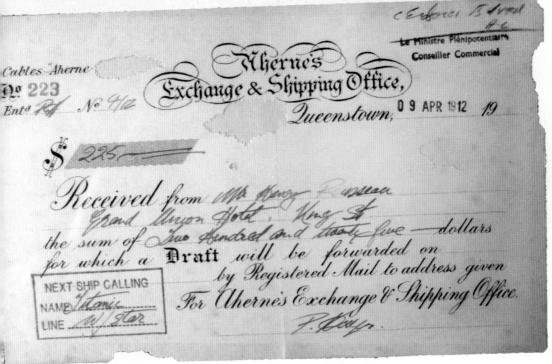

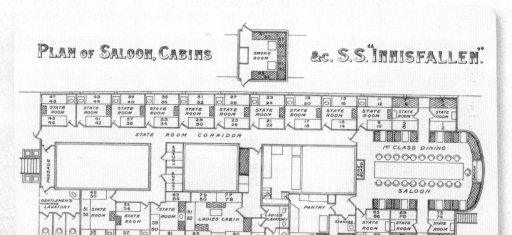

PLAN OF SALOON, CABINS &c. S.S. "INNISFALLEN".

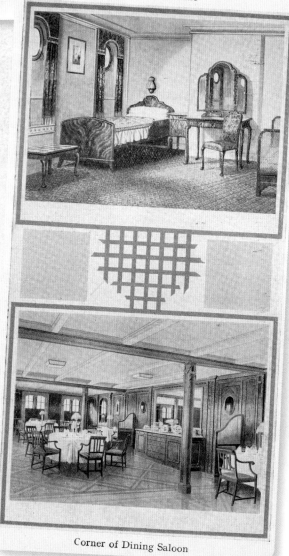

Cabin De-Luxe

A plan and interior images of the first *Innisfallen*, built in 1896 in Newcastle. She was sunk by the German submarine U-64 on 23 May 1918, whilst travelling from Liverpool to Cork. Ten lives were lost.

Corner of Dining Saloon

This photograph of the City of Cork Steam Packet Company dock was taken on 15 July 1938 and it shows the second *Innisfallen*, which first saw service in 1930 when it replaced the *Killarney*. On 21 December 1940 she hit a mine on the River Mersey, sinking with the loss of four crewmen.

This advertising postcard features the third *Innisfallen* on the Cork to Fishguard route. This ship came into service in 1948 and continued until the route moved from Fishguard to Swansea in 1969.

The *Inniscarra*, a two-funnelled steamship, was built in 1903 at Newcastle and it also serviced the Cork to Fishguard route. On 12 May 1918 she was torpedoed by the German submarine U-86 and sank with twenty-eight lives lost. There were five survivors: the captain, chief engineer and three crewmen.

S.S. "INNISCARRA" CORK & FISHGUARD DIRECT SERVICE. ARRIVAL AT CORK.

The SS *Ardmore* was built in 1909 by the Caledon Shipbuilding & Engineering Company of Dundee. The City of Cork Steam Packet cargo ship was torpedoed and sunk by German U-boat U-95 on 13 November 1917. The steamship was carrying general cargo on its voyage from London to Cork when it sank in the St Georges Channel.

An official advertisement for the City of Cork Steam Packet Company for the Cork International Exhibition. In addition to a pleasant sea voyage, the lakes of Killarney, Bantry Bay and Glengarriff could also be visited.

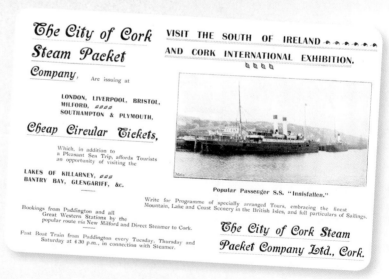

Overleaf: An official photograph of the City of Cork Steam Packet Company's docks and landing stage in Cork *c.* 1900. Carriages, wagons and hackneys await passengers and their luggage upon departure from the steamships. The hackney drivers charged a fixed fare for various destinations around the city and beyond.

Sketches

Pub. by A. D. Roche, Stationer, Cork.

View of Cork

The sketches reproduced here are various early views of Cork from rare illustrated guidebooks printed in London in 1872–73, newspapers and journals such as the *London Illustrated News* and the *Architect*, and by A. D. Roche. These early images are particularly useful for preserving the memory of streetscapes and the older Cork buildings which are now long gone. This 1857 view of Cork from the river is from Roche's six views of Cork. This scene bears remarkable similarities to the oil on canvas of a paddle steamer entering the port of Cork by George M. W. Atkinson from 1842.

hory Pinx.t   Eng.d by Newman & Co. 48, Watling St London.

the River.

The Exchange Building, which dates from 1708, was the most important commercial building within the city. The architect Twiss Jones was employed to design the building and no expense was spared. Because it was frequented by the rich merchants of the city the print trade flourished and this area became known as Booksellers' Row.

CORN EXCHANGE, CORK.

The old Corn Exchange building from a small booklet issued by Newman & Co. in 1873. Sir Thomas Howard designed it in 1833. This building was used for the first Cork National Exhibition in 1852 and it later became the City Hall.

The Savings' Bank & Corn Exchange Cork.

This sketch entitled 'The Savings Bank and Corn Exchange Cork' is from an extremely rare illustrated booklet published by A. D. Roche in 1857 before he became established as a Cork photographer. The Cork artist James Mahony was commissioned to draw these fine illustrations. He was well known for his famine sketches which appeared in the *London Illustrated News*.

An unusual detached river scene from the *London Illustrated News*, 1861. In the centre we have Shandon and the red-brick buildings of Camden Quay, a microcosm of Georgian Cork. On the river a small sailing craft is accompanied by two rowing boats.

This panoramic view of the city was sketched from the residence of the Mayor of Cork, John Daly, who resided on Sunday's Well Road. Artistic licence is used as the steeples of Cork's churches rise phoenix-like above the city and the tall sailing ships' masts are like matchsticks in the lower harbour.

Opposite: This beautiful coloured illustration of Patrick's Bridge and Patrick Street is from Nelson's *Pictorial Guide to the City of Cork*, dated to 1872. Elegant horse-drawn carriages and the paddle steamer on the left evoke thoughts of a more leisurely way of life.

The wide sweep of the South Mall with the Imperial Hotel's dedicated carriage arriving with weary passengers. The Victorian ladies in their elegant fashions stroll with gentlemen in their top hats along this commercial thoroughfare.

Opposite: An unusual foray into the postcard publishing world by the Cork printing firm of Purcell & Co. An artistic view was the chosen medium instead of photography. Proby's Bridge, Elizabeth Fort, Bishop's Street and St Finbarre's Cathedral were the selected subjects.

Registered
Purcell & Co Cork.

S. FINBAR'S CATHEDRAL,
CORK.

A scene of Patrick Street as it looks towards Patrick's Hill and Government House, printed in 1883. The beautiful, ornate, cast-iron lamp in the centre also had a water feature at its base, which was useful for providing water to thirsty people and horses alike.

The natural sweep of the river is very noticeable in this 1885 black and white sketch of Patrick Street, which was built over the river channel. Hackneys ply their trade whilst Cork's citizens adopt a leisurely pace of life.

This early postcard is known as a Gruss Aus type postcard and was issued before 1900. These cards often feature vignettes, in this case of Blarney Castle, and the buildings have an appearance of being drawn by a draftsman because of their very straight lines.

This animated postcard appears to be warning Corkonians of the impending dangers of the new tramway system of 1898. It forecasts pandemonium in the streets as these silent horseless carriages create havoc amidst cyclists, horses and swooning ladies.

ST. PATRICK'S STREET.

Dear Theo
Many thanks for card, and sorry you did not come over this afternoon I hope it was not owing to Flors illness. See you tomorrow afternoon. E.

This ornate Patrick Street postcard features a lady and a tram on Cork's most fashionable street. The royal procession of King Edward VII made its grand entrance through Patrick Street in 1903, about the time this postcard was published.

THE RIVER LEA & ST. MARY'S CATHEDRAL.

The River Lee with St Mary's, Pope's Quay, and St Anne's, Shandon, in the background. The river was widely fished by local fishermen at a time when stocks were plentiful. The embossed engraving of the Cork coat of arms adds to the character of this postcard.

CORK. FATHER MATHEW'S QUAY.

RK. S⊥ PATRICK STREET.

Raphael Tuck produced 'Tuck's Oillette Postcards' which were sold for one penny each in the early 1900s. They were very popular, like this scene of Patrick Street.

Above left: A view of the Holy Trinity Church on Charlotte Quay by Raphael Tuck. The ornate façade of the church had just been completed a few years before this illustration, which has a very soft-focus appeal.

Left: This beautiful illustration of the 1883 Exhibition Hall, purpose-built for the Cork Exhibition of that year, was published by the *Architect* in 1884. It also shows a new swing bridge, which was constructed in November 1882. This was built to replace the old Anglesea Bridge which, with the large volume of traffic then traversing Cork's streets, had outlived its usefulness.

ork has its fair share of magnificent architecture. Early images of some of the most iconic buildings, such as the old Provincial Bank which was nearing completion in the mid 1860s, St Anne's, Shandon, and St Finbarre's Cathedral are included here. However, some beautiful buildings have also been lost over time, including the old Opera House and Sutton's buildings, and only surviving photographs can provide an idea of the richness of architecture that has been lost.

Buildings

The old Provincial Bank before its completion in 1867 (note the scaffolding still in position). The beautiful wrought-iron work of Anglesea Bridge built in 1830 blends seamlessly with one of Cork's most beautiful buildings. The long exposure has resulted in ghostly images of passing people.

Previous page: The old County Jail was remodelled by the architects George and Richard Pain in 1818. Unfortunately it was deemed necessary by the authorities in University College Cork to demolish the buildings in the background in the 1950s and the replacement buildings clash with their surroundings.

The old City Hall and new Anglesea Bridge, later renamed Parnell Bridge, *c.* 1880s. The bridge is long gone, but the survival of photographs such as this presents a picture of how much this area has changed. Sailing ships had their cargoes discharged by dockers at the nearby quays, providing much-needed employment.

An unusual stereo view of Shandon and graveyard minus railings, dated 1877. The two statues, affectionately known as Bob and Joan, can be seen perched proudly on their respective pillars at the entrance to the Green Coat School.

Some of these early bow-fronted buildings still exist on the Grand Parade. No. 46, on the left of the picture, was the impressive Cork City & County Clubhouse. The notable architect Sir John Benson redesigned this building to give it a more striking appearance.

St Finbarre's Cathedral before its towers were erected (completed in 1877).
The exterior entrance arches had yet to be embellished by the stonemasons.
The financial outlay for constructing a building of this quality was a nightmare
for the clergy and worshippers alike to raise.

Queen's College, as it was named before the establishment of the National University of Ireland Act of 1908. Sir Thomas Deane and Benjamin Woodward designed the college, which first opened its doors to students in 1849 amidst much controversy – it was considered a 'Godless college' by the Catholic Church, which was given no say in its running.

A later image of the quadrangle of University College Cork. This photograph was professionally taken in 1954 and it was used for a commercial postcard.

The castle at Blackrock, now an observatory, has changed little since this photograph was taken around 1890. The old fishing boat in the foreground is evidence of Blackrock's thriving fishing industry at this time. In 1849 the Blackrock fishermen presented Queen Victoria with a salmon upon her arrival in Cork harbour.

This photograph was taken by local photographer Andrew Sheppard, who had his studio at Winthrop Street in the 1950s. The curve of these buildings is quite similar to the Catholic Young Men's Association building at Castle Street. Note that Moynihan's tailors are advertising a salvage sale whilst another sign advertises Swedish massages.

The old Cork Opera House, *c.* 1905, formerly the Athenaeum, was remodelled by C. J. Philips. It opened on 17 September 1877 with a production of *Our Boys* by H. J. Byron. One of the most striking features of the Opera House was its fine acoustics.

A privately taken photograph of the ruins of the old Opera House the morning after the fire on Monday 12 December 1955 which completely engulfed the building. The Christmas pantomime *Sleeping Beauty* was being rehearsed when the building was evacuated.

A busy South Mall street scene. The cars in this photograph date it to the early 1950s. Sutton's building to the right of the picture was destroyed by one of the worst fires in the city's history on 29 November 1963.

A Sutton's billhead dated 8 November 1950. This firm was one of the largest suppliers of coal to factories, businesses and householders. This invoice was addressed to Ogilvie & Moore, Parnell Place, and the order consisted of Polish coal, Welsh coal and slack.

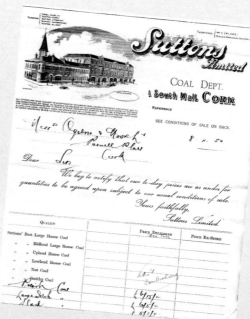

An architectural gem: the Queen Anne house on Bachelor's Quay, formerly the sheriffs' house. For many years it was affectionately known as the dolls house. Even though it was offered to the Cork Corporation for a token payment of one shilling, sadly it was demolished shortly after this photograph was taken.

It is hard to believe that this photograph was taken as late as January 1948 by Alec Day, a notable Cork photographer. It shows the Dickensian reading room of the Cork Commercial Buildings. This thirty-foot-high room was remodelled to create a new floor at the Imperial Hotel in March of that year.

Churches

Following the repeal of the penal laws under the act of Catholic Emancipation in 1829, the Catholic clergy were quick to respond by building new churches. Ss Peter and Paul's Church was built to replace the old chapel at Carey's Lane, the Holy Trinity Church was built on Father Mathew Quay, although it took many years for its beautiful spire to be completed, and the foundation stone for St Mary's on Pope's Quay was laid in 1832. The Protestant clergy were quick to respond by building the magnificent French Gothic cathedral of St Finbarre's. This unusual glass lantern view, taken from the grounds of the North Monastery around 1905, shows the Catholic cathedral of St Mary's and the Protestant church of St Anne's, Shandon. To their right the old Wise's Distillery chimney peeps out.

A technological marvel – a night scene captured by a camera in 1890! This glass lantern was hand coloured to reproduce a night-time scene. Church Street and Shandon reflect in the warm glow of the artificial light.

An unusual stereo view published by the Keystone Co. showing St Mary's and St Anne's around 1904. The darkened figures on the right blend into the background. The Firkin Crane building is on the left of this image.

An atmospheric view of Shandon, its tower dwarfing the skyline. One of the most photographed churches in the city, it is immortalised by Fr Prout's poem 'The Bells of Shandon'.

An interesting hand-coloured glass lantern slide of St Finbarre's from 1890. This type of photograph was hand coloured and then sandwiched between two glass plates. The artist appears to have taken a little artistic licence, as different types of stone appear on the towers. The initial budget for building the cathedral was a mere £15,000, but at the time of its completion by William Burges the costs had escalated to £100,000. By 1875 the project was in serious financial trouble, but generous donations of £10,000 by the brewer William Crawford and £20,000 by the distiller Francis Wise ensured its completion in 1877.

This image has been distorted. Although it looks like the same view, this in fact shows the opposite side of St Finbarre's to the previous picture, as demonstrated by the presence of the old gravestones. The huge towers of St Finbarre's have not been constructed yet, but the golden angel, a gift from the architect William Burges, is in place. This image is dated to *c.* 1870.

Opposite below: This is the prospectus for the rebuilding of St Finbarre's Cathedral – the subscribers' list reads like a who's who of Cork society.

Below: A *London Illustrated News* sketch of the foundation stone of St Finbarre's Cathedral being laid. The old cathedral in the background was demolished in 1865 to accommodate the building of the present cathedral. An ingenious mechanism on tracks was used to lay the extremely heavy foundation stone in place.

An early interior photograph of St Mary's, Pope's Quay, which dates to 1877. The photographer has captured the natural light, which must have involved an extremely long exposure time for this image.

This old Keystone Co. stereo view dates to 1903. The ship in the foreground could make its way as far as George's Quay to discharge its cargo. The ornate spire of the Holy Trinity Church had only been completed a few years previously.

An early stereo view of Francis Guy's bookshop shows that an archway once existed as an entrance to Ss Peter and Paul's church. The foundation stone of this church was laid on 15 August 1859.

A *London Illustrated News* sketch of the new church of Ss Peter and Paul's, *c.* 1866. The old chapel at Carey's Lane had become too small for the ever-increasing congregation. The celebrated English architect E. W. Pugin designed this Gothic church, although it was considered by some to be a little too ornate.

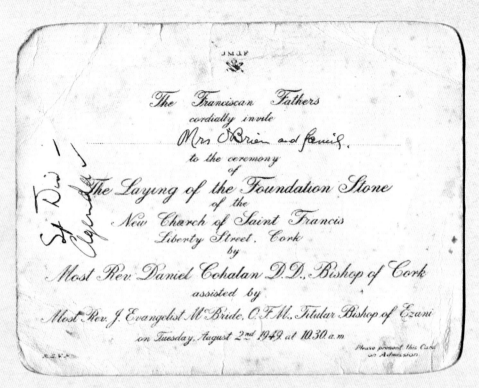

The Franciscan Fathers
cordially invite

Mrs O'Brien and family.

to the ceremony
of

The Laying of the Foundation Stone
of the
New Church of Saint Francis
Liberty Street, Cork
by

Most Rev. Daniel Cohalan D.D., Bishop of Cork

assisted by

Most Rev. J. Evangelist M'Bride, O.F.M., Titular Bishop of Ezani

on Tuesday, August 2nd 1949 at 10.30 a.m

Please present this Card
on Admission

An invitation card addressed to a Mrs O'Brien and family inviting them to attend the solemn laying of the foundation stone of St Francis' Church on Tuesday 2 August 1949. The old Liberty Street Church and surrounding alleyways were demolished to make way for the magnificent new building.

Rear View, Franciscan Church,
Liberty Street, Cork

This sketch from the architect Robert Walker is dated 24 February 1888 and shows a plan and an outside view of the Capuchin convent at Charlotte Quay, now Father Mathew Quay. Although this is called a convent, which would usually suggest that the building was inhabited by nuns, the Capuchins are a male order.

An aerial view of the North Chapel from 1887, with Murphy's Brewery chimney in the background. This was probably taken from St Anne's, Shandon. Curiously, the cathedral was wrongly identified as the Holy Trinity Church on Father Mathew Quay by the publisher.

Streetscapes

These streetscapes, many taken during the late nineteenth or early twentieth centuries, provide a fascinating record of both familiar and vanished aspects of life in Cork city. This is an unusual rooftop view of the Grand Parade from around 1880. To the right is No. 31 with a house and a church decorator occupying the building, whilst bicycles, which were becoming very popular at this time in Victorian Cork, were sold by its neighbour, Cooke's Cycle Depot.

Father Mathew has remained in more or less the same position but change has occurred all about him. The old Cork premises and lanes have disappeared and have been replaced by the Merchant's Quay Shopping Centre. Merchant's Street, where Roches Stores was founded, is long gone.

An early stereo view of Father Mathew's statue brings to mind the lines from a song: 'the smell from Patrick's Bridge is wicked, how does Father Mathew stick it? Here's up them all says the Boys of Fairhill.' The railings were erected to protect the statue and the rounded stone bollards were there to prevent cart wheels from coming too close.

A busy Patrick Street thoroughfare *c.* 1880, with hackney carriages in the foreground. These horse-drawn cabs had fixed fares: a journey to St Luke's Cross was sixpence whilst a journey to College Road was also sixpence, but for more than two people the price rose to ninepence.

Trams had been in existence for just a few years when these images were taken. The first is a sepia stereo view dated to 1903, whilst the second is a hand-coloured glass slide of the same image, which was republished in colour two years later.

Numerous hackneys vie for business in this Guy Company's photograph dating to 1896. Note the grossly overloaded cart with the driver perched precariously on top of the goods – the poor horse's legs must have been buckling from the weight he was pulling!

Hackneys, horse and carts, and a magnificent carriage outside Cash's department store dominate this Patrick Street scene which dates to *c.* 1910. Two barefoot boys to the right make their way gingerly across this busy street.

In this 1902 view two men appear to be working perilously close to the tramway system. They seem to be digging up cobblestones which were frequently used as a hardwearing road surface.

A very early albumen print of Patrick Street when horse-drawn transport was in the ascendancy, looking towards Cash's. To the extreme right the building is clad in slate, a feature of very early Cork architecture.

Opposite: An early William Lawrence albumen photograph of Patrick Street. The wonderful building of Woodford Bourne's can be seen at the far end of the street. The canopies on the shops next to Woodford Bourne's add a continental air to the scene. The slated buildings of Mollard & Co. and Henry Franks appear to be suffering from major subsidence problems – their windows are clearly sagging. This contrasts sharply with the beautiful Gothic arches on the building to the right of the picture.

Previous page: This albumen print predates the erection of the National Monument (unveiled on St Patrick's Day in 1906) and gives an unimpeded view of the streetscape of the Grand Parade, showing its uneven buildings with their unusual shop fronts and beautiful bow-fronted structures on the left. This is before the electric tramway. *Inset*: A black and white glass lantern view from around 1880. Fishing nets have been left hanging to dry on the iron railings on the near side of the river. The wide nature of the Grand Parade is very evident in this image.

Below: The South Mall was the nerve centre of Cork's financial and legal businesses. It still contains many Georgian buildings and beautiful architecture. By 1832 what remained of the river channel was covered over.

An early stereo view showing an all but deserted South Mall. The horse and cart was taking on water from the fire hydrant to dampen down the dusty street. Looking towards the very end of the street a ship's mast is visible near Parnell Bridge.

An unidentified Cork lane, possibly on the south side of the city. The cobbled walkway contrasts sharply with these old white-washed cottages. Two small girls play, one of them fascinated by the photographer's presence. A solitary lamp was the only available lighting for the whole street. Two chickens run free as the occupants peer curiously from their doorways.

This hand-coloured glass lantern slide was published by the Bureau of Visual Instruction, Chicago Public Schools. It dates to the early 1900s and is entitled 'Streets and cottages in the poor quarter of Cork'. This view shows Stephen Street off Barrack Street.

The handsome wrought-iron archway and cast pillars made by the Hive Iron Works provide the perfect backdrop to the magnificent tree-lined avenue of the Mardyke. Alas Dutch elm disease took its toll on the trees, but Fitzgerald's Park is still a favourite with Corkonians young and old.

To the right of this hand-coloured slide a beautiful ornate bandstand can be seen. The Mardyke was a place to see and hear some of the best brass and military bands in the city. At the time if you did not own a gramophone, piano or other musical instrument, the only way to hear music was to go to a live concert or a performance at your local bandstand.

MERCIER PRESS
Cork
www.mercierpress.ie

© Michael Lenihan, 2011

ISBN: 978 1 85635 882 8

10 9 8 7 6 5 4 3 2 1

A CIP record for this title is available from the British Library

Printed and bound in the EU.